Barriers

10 8
6 00

Linguistic Inquiry Monographs
Samuel Jay Keyser, general editor

Barriers

Noam Chomsky

The MIT Press
Cambridge, Massachusetts
London, England

Fifth printing, 1994

This book was set in VIP Times by Village Typographers, Inc., and printed and bound in the United States of America.

Library of Congress Cataloging-in-Publication Data

Chomsky, Noam.
  Barriers.

  (Linguistic inquiry monographs; 13)
  Bibliography: p.
  Includes index.
  1. Generative grammar. I. Title. II. Series.
P158.C485   1986   415   85-23776
ISBN 0-262-03118-3 (hardcover)
         0-262-53067-8 (paperback)

Contents

Series Foreword

We are pleased to present this monograph as the thirteenth in the series *Linguistic Inquiry Monographs*. These monographs will present new and original research beyond the scope of the article, and we hope they will benefit our field by bringing to it perspectives that will stimulate further research and insight.

Originally published in limited edition, the *Linguistic Inquiry Monograph* series is now available on a much wider scale. This change is due to the great interest engendered by the series and the needs of a growing readership. The editors wish to thank the readers for their support and welcome suggestions about future directions the series might take.

Samuel Jay Keyser
for the Editorial Board

Acknowledgments

I am indebted for helpful comments to Kyle Johnson, Howard Lasnik, Luigi Rizzi, and Esther Torrego, among others.

Barriers

Introductory Comments

I want to explore some rather murky questions concerning the theories of government and bounding, including, in particular, the possibility of a unified approach to these topics. The intuitive idea is that certain categories in certain configurations are barriers to government and to movement (application of the general rule Move-α). A natural speculation would be that the same categories are barriers in the two cases. As is well known, however, government is a stricter and "more local" relation. We might therefore expect that one barrier suffices to block government, whereas more than one barrier inhibits movement, perhaps in a graded manner. One of the questions I want to consider is whether there is a reasonable notion of barrier that has these properties.

The concept of government enters into a broad range of considerations; as a result, any proposal concerning its formulation has many and intricate consequences. Furthermore, many of the empirical phenomena that appear to be relevant are still poorly understood. With regard to the theory of movement, it appears that a number of different factors enter into informant judgments, including lexical choices to which they are sensitive; it is therefore necessary to proceed on the basis of some speculations concerning the proper idealization of complex phenomena, how they should be sorted out into a variety of interacting systems (some of which remain quite obscure), which ones may tentatively be put aside to be explained by independent (sometimes unknown) factors, and which others are relevant to the subsystems under investigation. I will consider several paths through the maze of possibilities that come to mind.

I will assume here the "principles and parameters" approach to linguistic theory outlined in Chomsky 1981 and related work; see Chomsky 1985 for some general background. In this conception, Universal Grammar (UG) is a system of subtheories, each with certain parameters of variation. A particular (core) language is determined by fixing parameters in these subtheories.

The idea that there should be a general unifying concept of locality that enters into various subdomains of UG has been pursued in a number of ways since it was proposed by Jan Koster (1978); see, among other works, Bouchard 1984, Culicover and Wilkins 1984. My specific concerns here are more modest, limited to government and bounding.

Because of the sometimes intricate connections among the various subtheories, small changes in the formulation of some principle or notion may have large-scale and wide-ranging consequences. Such problems will typically arise insofar as we eliminate specific rule systems in favor of systems determined by setting values of parameters of UG. This is naturally a positive development, one that is inherent in any serious effort to deepen explanatory power, but it also means that theoretical proposals face a far more difficult empirical challenge than in earlier work. Furthermore, arguments become more intricate as the options for selecting rule systems are reduced. Again, this is a positive development, but one that increases the difficulty of evaluating—or even determining—the consequences entailed by specific proposals.

---

1. X-Bar Theory

Let us begin with some questions concerning X-bar theory. Assume a distinction between lexical and nonlexical categories, where the lexical categories are based on the features [±N, ±V], yielding the categories Noun ([+N, −V]), Verb ([−N, +V]), Adjective ([+N, +V]), and Preposition-Postposition ([−N, −V]). The nonlexical categories include complementizer and INFL, the latter including Tense and Agreement elements and Modals. Assume that other categories are projections of these zero-level categories in terms of the following schemata (order parametrized; the choices here are for English, the convention I shall adopt throughout), where X* stands for zero or more occurrences of some maximal projection and $X = X^0$:[1]

(1)

a. $X' = X\ X''^*$

b. $X'' = X''^*\ X'$

I refer to X'' in (1a) as the complement of X (or X') and to X'' in (1b) as the specifier of X (or X', or X''); if X'' is an NP, then in (1a) it is the object of X and in (1b) the subject of X. The notions complement, specifier, object, and subject are relational or functional, not categorial: there are no categories with these labels. I omit consideration here of possible further structure and assume that the basic properties of phrase structure for particular languages are determined by fixing parameters of Case theory and θ-theory and by lexical properties.[2] I will use the conventional symbols NP, VP, AP, PP for the maximal projections (here assumed to be X'') of the lexical categories. The X-bar constraints are satisfied at D-Structure, but not at other levels of representation if adjunction has taken place in a derivation. The options for X''^* in (1) are drastically limited, by θ-theory in the case of complements; Kayne (1984) argues that the options for X''^* are zero or one. In any event, the number of possible realizations of the X-bar schemata is finite, in fact small.[3]

Given the conditions of X-bar theory in one or another of its variants, lexical entries can be limited to a minimal form with indication of no more than inherent and selectional features, and phrase structure rules can apparently be dispensed with entirely, a highly desirable move for familiar reasons.

Does this system extend to the nonlexical categories as well? Evidently, the optimal hypothesis is that it does. Let us assume this to be correct. Then the clausal categories conventionally labeled S and S' might be I'' and C'', respectively, where I = INFL and C = complementizer, as in (2):

(2)

a. $S = I'' = [NP\ [_{I'}[_{VP}\ V\ ...]]]$

b. $S' = C'' = [...\ [_{C'}\ C\ I'']]$

Other options for (2a) might include taking S to be V'', with V' replacing VP, or eliminating V' to produce a "flat" structure, yielding languages with quite different properties.[4] I will extend conventional notation for the lexical categories to the nonlexical ones as well, referring to the maximal projections C'' and I'' as CP and IP, respectively.

In general, specifiers are optional but the choice of complements is determined by the Projection Principle. Assume here that the specifier of IP (in (2a)) is required by the Extended Projection Principle.[5]

A technical question arises in the case where the specifier position is missing in a maximal projection X''. Is the structure (3a) or (3b) (skipping X')?

(3)
a. $[_{NP}[_{N'}[_N$ pictures] [of John]]]
b. $[_{NP}[_N$ pictures] [of John]]

Let us assume that in this case either (3a) or (3b) is possible: choice of X' is forced when there is a specifier, otherwise optional. Some empirical considerations bearing on this issue will be noted below.

2. Theory of Movement

Consider next the theory of movement. Assume that there are two types of movement: substitution and adjunction. Substitution has the following general properties:

(4)
a. There is no movement to complement position.
b. Only X^0 can move to the head position.
c. Only a maximal projection can move to the specifier position.
d. Only minimal and maximal projections (X^0 and X'') are "visible" for the rule Move-α.

Property (4a) follows from the θ-Criterion. Property (4b) would follow from an appropriate form of Emonds's Structure-Preserving Hypothesis (Emonds 1976), as would (4c) on the X-bar theoretic assumption that heads cannot be base-generated without a maximal projection so that a bare head cannot appear in the specifier position to receive a moved X^0 category.

It follows that apart from X^0-movement to head position, substitution will always move a maximal projection to the specifier position. The two major cases will be NP-movement to the subject of IP (= S) or NP and *wh*-movement to the specifier of CP (= S'). Movement to head position is narrowly constrained by the interaction of principles of UG, one major case being movement of V to I, forming the inflected verb V_I, with possible subsequent movement of V_I to C (see section 11).

Assume that movement is never determined by specific rule, but rather results from the interaction of other factors in the manner described in the references cited above. Thus, Case considerations will be involved in determining NP-movement, morphological properties require V-raising to I, and we may assume that general properties of scope determine the position of *wh*-phrases at LF: specifically, these phrases are not adjoined to IP but are in the pre-IP position with scope over IP, what is usually called "movement to COMP." This condition may be stated precisely in a number of different ways, with differing consequences. It might be a condition on LF. That is, perhaps general properties of LF require that *wh*-phrases (and other similar elements, for example, empty operators) appear in one of the D-Structure-determined positions: they are either generated at D-Structure in pre-IP position or moved to such a position by substitution, this position being occupied at D-Structure by an appropriate empty category to create a target position for substitution; choice of this category can be regarded as what triggers choice of pied-piping or P-stranding under the Structure-Preserving Hypothesis. Another possibility is that *wh*-phrases have clausal scope for general reasons and cannot be adjoined to IP; hence, they must move to the position of specifier of CP (adjunction to CP being excluded for reasons to which I return directly). The latter approach blocks even intermediate adjunction of *wh*-phrases and the like to IP. There is some reason to believe that this stronger condition is required, and I will henceforth assume it.[6] As a result, although the rule of quantifier raising QR may involve adjunction to IP, this option is barred for operators of the *wh*-phrase type.

One consequence of these rather natural assumptions is that S' (= CP) is not a "defective category" with regard to X-bar theory, having its maximal projection at the X' level, but rather falls into the general pattern. Another is that *wh*-movement is not "movement to COMP" as typically construed, but rather is movement to the position of specifier of CP. This conclusion has a number of further consequences. One is that the complementizer C remains a "free agent" after *wh*-movement: it can delete, cliticize onto an adjacent word, and so forth, all of which should strictly speaking not be possible if it is within an adjoined structure formed by *wh*-movement. Furthermore, it is not problematic that *wh*-movement is to the left even if the complementizer is on the right, as Hilda Koopman observes; see Koopman 1984 for examples. Finally, consider what can appear (apart from C) in pre-IP position in a clause. The only possibilities are as in (5), where X″ might be a *wh*-phrase or other element subject to the same LF conditions (perhaps an empty operator) and V_I is an inflected verbal element:[7]

(5)
$[_{CP}$ (X″) (V_I) IP]

This is an essential part of the verb-second phenomenon found in many languages. Its basic properties follow from X-bar theory if we extend the system (1) to nonlexical categories and adopt the general assumptions just sketched. It follows that of the three elements that might appear in pre-IP position—namely, inflected verb, *wh*-phrase (or similar element), and complementizer—only two may appear: one in the specifier position and one in the head position. This descriptive principle, here derived primarily from X-bar theory, is supported by a range of empirical phenomena, as shown by Rizzi (1984).

In short, these assumptions about X-bar theory and movement seem plausible on both conceptual and empirical grounds.

Consider next adjunction. I will assume the following principle concerning adjunction:[8]

(6)
Adjunction is possible only to a maximal projection (hence, X″) that is a nonargument.

In particular, adjunction to NP or CP is ruled out when these are arguments, and adjunction to VP is allowed, a possibility that will be exploited below.

Koopman and Sportiche (1982) argue in support of VP-adjunction at LF on the basis of properties of QR: thus, if the object adjoins to IP in (7a) yielding (7b), *everyone* will locally bind *he* as well as its own trace, violating the Bijection Principle, but this will not be the case if the object adjoins to VP, yielding (7c):[9]

(7)
a. everyone$_i$ likes someone he$_i$ met
b. everyone$_i$ $[_{IP}$[someone he$_i$ met]$_j$ $[_{IP}$ t$_i$ likes t$_j$]]
c. everyone$_i$ $[$t$_i$ $[_{VP}$[someone he$_i$ met]$_j$ $[_{VP}$ likes t$_j$]]]

May (1985) draws the same conclusion on the basis of examples such as (8a–b):

(8)

a. who does everyone like

b. who likes everyone

In (8a) either *who* or *everyone* may have wide scope, but in (8b) only *who* may have wide scope. May argues that in the case of (8a) the rule QR, which adjoins the quantifier to IP, yields (9), whereas in the case of (8b) it yields either (10a) or (10b), depending on whether adjunction is to IP or VP:

(9)

who_i does $[_{IP}$ $everyone_j$ $[_{IP}$ e_j like $e_i]]$

(10)

a. who_i $[_{IP}$ $everyone_j$ $[_{IP}$ e_i likes $e_j]]$

b. who_i $[_{IP}$ e_i $[_{VP}$ $everyone_j$ $[_{VP}$ likes $e_j]]]$

May then adds the crucial general assumption (12), which I will adopt, concerning adjunction structures: namely, in a structure of the form (11), a typical adjunction structure with α adjoined to β, α is not dominated by the category β; rather, β consists of two "segments," and a category is dominated by β only if it is dominated by both of these segments:[10]

(11)

$[_\beta$ α $[_\beta$ ...]]

(12)

α is dominated by β only if it is dominated by every segment of β.

In (9) *who* and *everyone* are dominated by exactly the same maximal projections (namely, the clause CP). Under this condition, May argues, the quantifier phrases commute; either scope gives a permissible interpretation. In (10b) *everyone* is dominated by the maximal projection IP, which does not dominate *who,* so *who* has wider scope; note that *everyone* still has scope over IP, since it is not dominated by VP. The structure (10a) arguably violates the Superiority Condition and hence violates the Empty Category Principle (ECP) if the Superiority Condition reduces to the ECP, with the subject trace not "locally" governed. But in any case it is an ungrammatical form. The only interpretation of (8b), then, is (10b), with *who* having wide scope, whereas either scope order is possible in interpreting (8a).

If these arguments are correct, then we have empirical support for allowing the option of adjunction to VP. In the subsequent discussion I will assume the principle (6) concerning adjunction and May's assumption (12) concerning the interpretation of adjunction structures such as (11). The theory-internal arguments just sketched lend empirical support to these assumptions, but nothing that follows depends on their correctness.

To summarize, I am assuming that X-bar theory with the basic form (1) is generalized to nonlexical categories and that the principles (4) and (6) hold for movement, along with May's assumption (12) concerning the interpretation of adjunction structures.

3. Government

Let us turn next to the notions of c-command and government, giving first a schematic characterization, with refinements to be investigated as we proceed. Putting aside adjunction structures such as (11) for the moment, we may understand "c-command" in a general way as follows:[11]

(13)
α c-commands β iff α does not dominate β and every γ that dominates α dominates β.

Where γ is restricted to maximal projections (following Aoun and Sportiche 1983), we will say that α *m-commands* β.[12] It seems that for the binding theory, γ should be taken to be any branching category, along the lines of Reinhart 1976; otherwise, for example, *the city's* [*destruction t*] would be a condition C violation and *its* [*destruction t*] a condition B violation.

Consider next the notion of government. The intuitive idea we will pursue is that α governs β if α m-commands β and there is no barrier γ that dominates β but not α, where the notion of barrier must still be made precise. Thus, a barrier will "protect" β from being governed by α, which m-commands it:

(14)
α governs β iff α m-commands β and every barrier for β dominates α.

In general, then, in the configuration (15) α will not govern β if γ is a barrier for β:

(15)

...α...[$_\gamma$ ...β...]

The next question is, What is a barrier? Before proceeding to this question, let us return again to adjunction structures such as (11):

(16)

...δ...[$_\gamma$ α [$_\gamma$ ...β...]]

Given the assumption (12) about adjunction structures, in (16) γ does not dominate α. Furthermore, in (16) α c-commands β but not conversely, since γ dominates β but not α. We also have the (perhaps unwanted) consequence that α c-commands the category γ and conversely. It is simple enough to avoid this by resorting to the concept "exclude" defined directly below, but since it seems that no empirical consequences ensue, I will leave (13) unchanged.

Suppose now that in (16) γ is a barrier for β. According to the definition just given, α does not govern β, since there is a barrier—namely, γ—that dominates β but not α. If in fact α should govern β in this case, then the definition of "government" must be slightly revised. Let us say that in (16) δ *excludes* α but γ does not:

(17)

α excludes β if no segment of α dominates β.

Then in (16) γ does not exclude α, but α excludes γ and δ excludes and is excluded by both α and γ: δ is entirely disconnected from α, γ.

We now define "government" in terms of exclusion rather than domination:

(18)

α governs β iff α m-commands β and there is no γ, γ a barrier for β, such that γ excludes α.

Apart from adjunction structures, the definitions of "government" in terms of exclusion and domination coincide. They differ in that according to (18) α governs β in (16) but according to (14) it does not. We will return to some empirical considerations bearing on this matter, which suggest that the definition (18) in terms of "exclusion" is the correct one.

4. Barriers

Let us turn now to determining what constitutes a barrier. Several concepts of government have been explored in the literature. These may be construed in terms of the way they select what counts as a barrier for β in (15), repeated here:

(15)
$$\ldots\alpha\ldots[_\gamma \ldots\beta\ldots]$$

In one conception γ might be any maximal projection; thus, β is protected from government by a maximal projection γ containing it. A second conception involves "minimality": α does not govern β in (15) if there is a "closer governor." Thus, if δ governs β in (19), then α does not govern β even if it otherwise satisfies the conditions for government:

(19)
$$\ldots\alpha\ldots[_\gamma \ldots\delta\ldots\beta\ldots]$$

Suppose, for example, that δ is an X^0 category that is the head of $\gamma = \delta'$, so that (19) is of the form (20):

(20)
$$\ldots\alpha\ldots[_{\gamma'} \ldots\gamma^0\ldots\beta\ldots]$$

In this case γ' is the barrier blocking government even though it is not a maximal projection.

Each of these intuitive ideas has been pursued in several versions; each has a certain naturalness. It would be reasonable to expect that the Minimality Condition will be relevant only to the theory of government, not to the theory of movement, since its essential function is to reduce ambiguity of government, a factor not relevant to the theory of movement. Let us therefore explore the possibility that barriers in the sense of the Minimality Condition are relevant only to the theory of government, whereas barriers in the first sense are relevant to the theory of government and movement, along the lines of the introductory remarks.

Let us restrict attention now to the first notion of government, returning later to the Minimality Condition, and ask how we should define "barrier" so that the definition (18) (or (14)) will have the desired properties.

Consider the sentence *John decided to see the movie,* with the structure (21):

(21)

John decided [$_{CP}$ e [$_{IP}$ PRO to [$_{VP}$ see the movie]]]

Here, it must be the case that *decide* does not govern either PRO or *the movie,* so either CP or IP is a barrier to government.

Let us consider first whether either CP or IP is an *inherent* barrier to government, as would be suggested by the familiar conception described earlier, with maximal projections serving as barriers (recall that we are assuming that IP and CP—S and S′, respectively—are maximal projections). We know that IP cannot be an inherent barrier to government, assuming standard analyses of Exceptional Case-marking and raising, so the question reduces to the status of CP.

Can CP be an inherent barrier to government? Here too the answer appears to be negative. Kayne (1984) provides evidence that the category we are considering to be the specifier of CP can be governed from outside, just as the specifier of IP can be. Moreover, Belletti and Rizzi (1981) have argued that the head of NP can also be governed from outside; hence, presumably the head of CP (namely, C) can be as well. The same conclusion follows from the analysis of Stowell (1981) (see also Saito 1984) that takes presence of complementizer to depend on government of the head of CP.[13] Hence, we may tentatively conclude that if α governs β, it also governs the specifier and head of β; in particular, that CP is not an absolute barrier to government.

The analysis of the ECP developed by Lasnik and Saito (1984), which I shall generally follow here, also entails that CP is not an inherent barrier to government and that what we are now taking to be the specifier of CP can be governed from outside CP. Consider the following typical paradigm, where only the traces of the wide-scope *wh*-phrase are indicated:[14]

(22)

a. how did John want [$_{CP}$ t′ [$_{IP}$ to fix the car t]]
b. *how did John know [$_{CP}$ which car [$_{IP}$ to fix t]]
c. which car did John know [$_{CP}$ how [$_{IP}$ to fix t]]
d. *how did Bill wonder [$_{CP}$ who [$_{IP}$ wanted [t′ [to fix the car t]]]]

Assuming the Lasnik-Saito analysis, (22b) is barred by failure of antecedent government. But the trace *t* in (22d) is antecedent-governed exactly as in (22a), so it must be that t' is the "offending trace"; antecedent government fails to hold of the pair (how, t') in (22d). We must then assume that t' is not properly governed by *want* even if it is governed by *want*. Note further that antecedent government fails for the pair (how, t') in (22d) for the same reason that it fails to hold of the pair (how, t) in (22b). In both (22b) and (22d) the intervening CP is a barrier to government, but in (22a) it is not, since t' is antecedent-governed (hence, governed) in (22a). It therefore follows that CP cannot be an inherent barrier to government and that the specifier of CP can be governed from outside of CP, assuming antecedent government to be a species of government.

The preceding discussion suggests that neither CP nor IP (nor, assuming the natural generalization, any maximal projection) is an *inherent* barrier to government. In (21) CP is a barrier for PRO but not for *e*. CP is a barrier for t' in (22d) and for t in (22b), but not for t' in (22a). We therefore have two plausible options to pursue: (i) two maximal projections constitute a barrier—hence, CP and its constituent IP in (22b,d)—but government across one maximal projection is permissible; (ii) one such category constitutes a barrier, but a category is a barrier only in some relative sense. The two approaches yield somewhat different consequences as they are developed in conjunction with the Minimality Condition, though they are not easy to distinguish empirically; we will return to the matter briefly in section 12. Much of the following discussion is independent of the choice between these alternatives. I will assume here the second approach, which generalizes to bounding theory along the lines of the introductory remarks and receives some empirical support, as we shall see in section 12.

Pursuing this idea, let us suppose that CP *inherits* barrierhood from IP, so that CP will be a barrier for something within IP but not for something in the pre-IP position. Then in (21), for example, CP will be a barrier for government of PRO by *decide* but not for government of *e* by *decide*, and the desired properties of (22) will also follow. Our definition of "barrier" will be relational: a category α will be a barrier for β for certain choices of β but not for others; a category may be a barrier by inheritance or intrinsically.

Furthermore, a potential barrier may be exempted from barrierhood by an appropriate relation to a lexical head. Thus, a category β θ-marked by α will be a barrier only by inheritance, not inherently. To formulate this idea properly requires some care; we cannot express it in terms of government, since the concept of barrier will enter into defining "government." Rather, we must express the relevant relation between a lexical head and the category in question in independent terms. Let us proceed by first developing the relevant relation between a head and a category being considered for barrierhood, then expressing in these terms the notion of barrier that enters into the theories of government and bounding.

Of the various kinds of relations that hold among elements, three appear to be relevant to the theories of government and bounding: (i) the relation between a zero-level category (a head) and the phrases to which it assigns some feature (θ-role or Case), (ii) the relation of agreement (as between subject and I (= INFL)), and (iii) the relation between elements in a link of a chain. Let us refer to the first relation as "head marking" and to the third as "chain coindexing." Where the head is a lexical category, we will refer to head marking as "lexical marking." Some relation based on lexical marking, to be determined as we proceed, is relevant to the definition of "barrier" for the theories of government and bounding; we will refer to this relation as "L-marking." Chain coindexing enters here only into the definition of proper government (the ECP). Agreement appears to enter into determination of both barriers and proper government.

Let us consider the relations that enter into L-marking, beginning with θ-marking. θ-marking meets a condition of "sisterhood" that is expressible in terms of X-bar theory, independently of government: a zero-level category α *directly θ-marks* β only if β is the complement of α in the sense of X-bar theory. It is only this form of θ-marking that is relevant to L-marking, not indirect θ-marking of the subject of a clause by its main verb, mediated, we assume, through the VP along lines discussed in Chomsky 1981, Marantz 1984.

We might extend the definition of "direct θ-marking" to include θ-marking of subject by VP. Given our assumptions about the structure of clauses, we would carry out this extension in terms of a specific notion of "sisterhood" that takes VP to be a sister of the subject of its clause even though I' dominates VP but not the subject. Suppose we say that α and β are *sisters* (in the relevant sense) if they are dominated by the same lexical projections; this notion is similar but not identical to government. Then a condition on θ-marking will be that the θ-marker and the recipient of the θ-role be sisters, where the θ-marker may be a head or a maximal projection. Note that if we define "sisterhood" in terms of lexical projections, as above, it follows that the subject is only indirectly θ-marked by the verbal head of a clause or gerund or by the head of a nominal, as in (23):

(23)
John's [$_{N'}$ refusal of the offer]

If we were to define "sisterhood" in terms of maximal rather than lexical projections, then we would have direct θ-marking in the case of (23).

Note that if V has a clausal complement CP (= C IP), then IP is a sister of V as "sisterhood" was just defined. Nevertheless, V does not θ-mark IP. We can, in fact, allow this possibility, since if V mistakenly θ-marks IP a θ-Criterion violation will result, since the argument CP will not receive a θ-role.

We therefore construe direct θ-marking as follows:

(24)
α directly θ-marks β only if α and β are sisters.

To sharpen these concepts, we would have to specify more closely the mechanisms of θ-marking (is it optional or obligatory, etc.) and some other matters. We would also have to work out precisely the mechanisms of "indirect θ-marking" of a subject by the V head of VP or the N head of NP. These issues will not arise here, so I will put the questions aside, restricting attention to direct θ-marking and assuming for concreteness that it is obligatory.[15]

Returning to L-marking, we may now tentatively identify it as direct θ-marking by a lexical category.

Let us turn now to the concept of barrier. We first define "blocking category" (BC) as in (25) and then define "barrier" in terms of BC as in (26):

(25)
γ is a BC for β iff γ is not L-marked and γ dominates β.

(26)
γ is a barrier for β iff (a) or (b):
a. γ immediately dominates δ, δ a BC for β;
b. γ is a BC for β, $\gamma \neq$ IP.

We understand γ in (25) and (26) to be a maximal projection, and we understand "immediately dominate" in (26a) to be a relation between maximal projections (so that γ immediately dominates δ in this sense even if a nonmaximal projection intervenes). In case (26a) the category γ inherits barrierhood from a BC that it dominates; in case (26b) γ is a barrier intrinsically, by virtue of its own status as a BC.

The exception for IP would be removed, simplifying (26b), if we were to assume that C L-marks its IP complement. This seems implausible, and we will see below that the "defective" character of IP apparently carries over to I'. I will leave (26) in the form given, though little that follows turns on the issue.

The definition of BC is based on an insight of Cattell (1976), subsequently developed in various ways by Kayne, Huang, Pesetsky, Longobardi, and others, concerning the role of government in permitting movement. Note that we are regarding IP as a "defective" category; it can only become a barrier by inheritance (that is, by (26a)), not simply by being a BC itself. We will turn later to various low-level parameters for IP and CP, relating only to bounding theory. Note that direct θ-marking by a head is a subvariety of government—in fact, the "core case" of government. It might be called "θ-government" (without circularity):[16]

(27)
α θ-governs β iff α is a zero-level category that θ-marks β, and α, β are sisters.

We tentatively construe "L-marking" as follows:

(28)
α L-marks β iff α is a lexical category that θ-governs β.

The categories NP and CP have often been held to play a special role in the theories of bounding and government, just as they do in binding theory. In the latter case it appears that the relevant feature is not a categorial one distinguishing NP and CP from others but rather the presence of a subject, hence of a "complete functional complex" with all functional roles satisfied; see Chomsky 1981, 1985. In the definitions above, no special stipulation was introduced distinguishing NP and CP from other maximal projections, but the distinction still is stipulated. As we shall see in more detail below, the distinction is shifted from the definition of "barrier" to a condition on adjunction (see (6)). If this move is correct, the next step would be to motivate this condition on adjunction.

We might motivate this condition in terms of θ-theory (modifying slightly a suggestion made by Kyle Johnson). Consider again an adjunction structure (29), where $\gamma = \beta$ and β is an argument:

(29)

$[_\gamma \; \alpha \; [_\beta \; ...]]$

Here β might be assumed to be "invisible" to θ-marking since it is not a full category but rather a segment of the two-segment category (γ, β) formed by the adjunction rule and thus not a recipient of a θ-role. As Probal Dasgupta points out (personal communication), we will then want to distinguish a structure (29) formed by adjunction from one that is base-generated, specifically, a small clause with β the "head" of γ ($= \beta$ in the theory of Stowell 1983). Looking at the matter slightly differently, we might assume that where the structure (29) is formed by an adjunction operation, then β is no longer the head of the construction, so that there is no "percolation" of θ-marking from γ to β. If assumptions along these lines prove tenable, then adjunction to an argument will always yield a violation of the θ-Criterion.

Given the concept of barrier defined above, let us return to (21):

(21)

John decided $[_{CP} \; e \; [_{IP} \; PRO \; to \; [_{VP} \; see \; the \; movie]]]$

Here CP is not a barrier for government of *e* by *decide,* but it is a barrier for government of PRO (and *the movie*) by *decide,* by (26b), since it inherits barrierhood in this case from IP, which is a BC.

---

5. Proper Government

The concept of government enters into virtually every subsystem of UG. It plays a special role in licensing empty categories in accordance with the ECP, which requires that every trace must be properly governed, a stronger relation than government. This principle has been developed in a variety of ways. I will take as a starting point here the theory of Lasnik and Saito (1984). In this conception the ECP does not hold of the pronominal elements PRO and pro or any empty operator, but it does hold of A-bound and $\bar{\text{A}}$-bound trace and, if Stowell (1981) is correct, the empty head of CP. A wide range of considerations bear on this distinction, and there is also a conceptual question as to how to formulate it. Let us assume, for concreteness, that empty categories are specified at D-Structure in terms of the features [±anaphoric], [±pronominal] and that these features (like others) do not change in the course of a derivation. Assume further that at D-Structure an empty category (apart from the empty complementizer) must be [+pronominal] and that trace may be assigned any features, the choice being determined by the interaction of principles of UG. Then the ECP will hold at LF (perhaps elsewhere) of any empty category that is nonpronominal (that is, not [+pronominal]): thus, of any empty category introduced in the course of a derivation as an anaphor, a variable, or the head of CP. We will return in section 11 to a different view of the matter.

So construed, the ECP states that a nonpronominal empty category must be *properly governed,* where "proper government" is defined as follows:

(30)
β is properly governed by α if it is governed by α and a certain kind of connection holds between α and β.

Let us tentatively take the connection to be θ-government or antecedent government. Antecedent government holds of a link (α,β) of a chain, where α governs β. We express the chain relation by coindexing.[17] We might express θ-marking in terms of feature sharing between a maximal projection and the θ-grid of the category that θ-marks it, following Stowell (1981). I will assume, however, that feature sharing through θ-marking and chain coindexing are different relations. Assume further that the index associated with a category is unique, whereas head marking may involve several Case features or θ-features.

We now have the following concept of proper government:

(31)
α properly governs β iff α θ-governs or antecedent-governs β.

In particular, an object is properly governed by its head, but a subject or adjunct can only be properly governed in a chain by antecedent government, so that subjects and adjuncts should in general behave alike under the ECP in a language with the X-bar structure to which we are limiting attention here (see Huang 1982). For concreteness, let us assume further the mechanism proposed by Lasnik and Saito (1984) for determining satisfaction of the ECP. We say that α assigns the feature [+γ] to β if it properly governs β and that β receives the feature [−γ] if it is not properly governed, where γ-marking, once assigned, is permanent. γ-marking takes place at S-Structure for elements of chains terminating in A-positions and at LF for elements in chains terminating in $\overline{\text{A}}$-positions, perhaps as a consequence of the Projection Principle in some manner. To satisfy the ECP, a nonpronominal empty category must have the marking $[+\gamma]$ at LF.

Let us return now to (22d):

(22)

d. *how did Bill wonder [$_{CP}$ who wanted [t' [to fix the car t]]]

Two questions arise: Why is t properly governed by t' (as t is properly governed by *how* in (22a))? Why is t' not properly governed? Let us put aside the first question for a moment and turn to the second, considering more closely just what is involved.

The element t' appears in the structure (32), adding categories suppressed in (22d):

(32)

want [$_{CP}$ t' [$_{C'}$ e IP]]

The various government relations that should hold are (33a–c) and perhaps (33d):

(33)

a. *Want* θ-governs CP.
b. *Want* governs both t' and e.
c. *Want* does not properly govern t'.
d. *Want* properly governs e, the head of CP.

Case (33a) is unproblematic, and (33b) follows since there is no barrier protecting either empty category from government by *want*. As Lasnik and Saito argue, (33c) is required; otherwise, the sentence (22d) would be grammatical. It follows here since *want* does not θ-govern t'. Similar considerations arise in "super-raising" constructions such as (34):

(34)

*John seems [$_{CP}$ that it is certain [$_{IP}$ t to win]]

Here *certain* governs but does not properly govern t, the trace of *John*, and antecedent government is blocked (at least) by CP, so the sentence violates the ECP.[18]

Case (33d) is required under Stowell's theory concerning empty complementizers. This consequence might be attributed to the principle of X-bar theory that a head and its projections share all properties apart from bar level, including the features involved in θ-marking. If we interpret θ-marking as the sharing of a feature between a category β and the θ-grid of its θ-marker α, then the relation will hold between the head of β and α as well. Thus, although *want* governs both the specifier t' and the head e of CP, it only θ-marks and hence properly governs e, as required.

Recall that we must ensure that an appropriate locality relation holds between β and its θ-governor α, and that we cannot appeal to government to express this condition since this concept is defined in terms of direct θ-marking. Before, we construed θ-government in terms of sisterhood, a concept of X-bar theory, but now we have a slight extension of this concept in terms of feature sharing between a head and its maximal projection; thus, the head of a sister of α is not a sister of α. This requires adding the qualification (35) to the Sisterhood Condition on θ-government, which was defined in (27):

(27)
α θ-governs β iff α is a zero-level category that θ-marks β, and α, β are sisters,

(35)
or β is the head of a sister of α.

The fact that this qualification is necessary raises doubts about (22d) and about the idea of explaining the distribution of the empty complementizer in terms of proper government. Nothing further turns on the question in the discussion here, apart from considerations that arise in section 11. I will keep the qualification (35) separate from the definition (27) of θ-government, returning to the matter in section 11.

Let us now turn to the first question raised concerning (22d): Why is t properly governed by t'? Exactly the same question arises with regard to *how* and its trace in (36):

(36)
how did [$_{IP}$ you [$_{VP}$ fix the car] t]

In both cases the matter is straightforward. There is only one BC that includes the trace but not its antecedent—namely, IP—but this is not a barrier (see (26b)).

I have assumed here that the D-Structure position of *how* in (36) (similarly in the other examples) is not within VP. Otherwise, movement would cross VP, which, not being L-marked, is a barrier to government and hence to proper government. Suppose however that the adjunct is within VP, as in (37) (with perhaps further internal structure in the VP):

(37)
how did [$_{IP}$ you [$_{VP}$ fix the car t]]

This possibility might be suggested, for example, by VP-movement structures such as *John wanted to fix the fender with a crowbar, and fix it that way, he did*. If so, then *wh*-movement of these adjuncts should always yield an ECP violation, since VP intervenes. Let us put off the matter for the moment, assuming that the analysis (36) is possible at least as an option—although, as we shall see, this does not resolve the issue.

Consider more closely the relation of I to its complement VP. We assume that I, not being a lexical category, does not L-mark VP (see (28)). Therefore, VP is a BC and a barrier. But VP is governed by I. If, furthermore, VP is θ-marked by I, then it is properly governed by I.[19] That this may be correct is suggested by such examples as (38):

(38)
fix the car, I wonder whether he will t

Here VP-extraction crosses a *wh*-island so that if its trace (like all traces) must be properly governed, it must be θ-marked by *will* since it is not antecedent-governed. I will assume that I does θ-mark its complement. (The matter becomes relevant only in section 11.) Note again that, not being lexical, I does not L-mark its VP complement.

The theory of barriers just outlined interacts with the theory of small clauses. Suppose we assume the theory proposed by Stowell (1983). Then a typical small clause construction would have the form (39):

(39)
they consider [$_\alpha$ John [$_{AP}$ intelligent]]

Here α is a projection of *intelligent* and *John* is its subject, receiving its θ-role from the AP "head" of α. Since *consider* Case-marks *John,* we must assume that α is not a barrier for Case-marking, hence not a barrier for government if Case-marking takes place under government. For this reason, it was assumed in Chomsky 1981 that "bar reduction" takes place as in "S'-deletion" constructions so that α is a nonmaximal projection of the category A. Now, however, we need not make that assumption. Since *consider* θ-marks α, α is not a barrier for its immediate constituents and can be taken to be AP. The same conclusion holds more generally.

Notice however that *consider* does not θ-mark the subject of the small clause, *John,* in (39). Nevertheless, the subject of a small clause must leave a properly governed trace under $\bar{\text{A}}$-movement since it can extract over a *wh*-island, as in (40), resulting in at most a weak *Wh*-Island Condition violation, not a strong ECP violation:

(40)

who did they wonder whether to consider [t (to be) intelligent]

As the example indicates, the same problem arises in Exceptional Case-marking constructions. Compare (41), which we have assumed to be an ECP violation (see (34)):

(41)

*John seems that it is considered [t to be intelligent]

In (41) *t* is neither antecedent-governed by *John* nor θ-marked by *consider,* so it is not properly governed and an ECP violation results. But in (40) we are forced to the conclusion that *t* is in fact properly governed.

One obvious difference between the two constructions lies in Case assignment: in (40) *consider* assigns Case to the trace *t* but in (41) it does not, Case having been "absorbed" in the passive construction. An analysis of the distinction in these terms (following, in essence, Lasnik and Saito 1984) may be possible, with a slight modification of the notions defined above. But there is a straightforward approach requiring no modifications—namely, an approach that assumes successive cyclic movement of *who* to VP in (40), then to its position in the matrix CP. This would yield the substructure (42):

(42)

[$_{\text{VP}}$ t' [$_{\text{VP}}$ consider [t ...

Nothing bars this process, as long as *who* is licensed at LF by appearing in clausal specifier position, and we have seen some reason to suppose that adjunction to VP is an option at least for LF-movement. In the structure (42) *t'* governs (hence, properly governs) *t,* if we adopt the definition of government (18) in terms of exclusion; there is no barrier that dominates *t* and excludes *t'*. Hence, independent of questions of Case, *t* is properly governed in (40) if VP-adjunction is permitted; and the status of *t'* is irrelevant for the ECP, under the Lasnik-Saito analysis, since it may be deleted at LF after having licensed *t* at S-Structure.

A similar process of VP-adjunction is barred for (41) under standard assumptions blocking "improper movement."[20]

Let us now consider the second possibility, namely, that the relevant distinction between (40) and (41) is in terms of Case—in other words, that Case-marking by a lexical category plays the same role as direct θ-marking in the theory of government. There are two cases, which we will examine in turn: the consequences for proper government and the consequences for the determination of BCs (hence, barriers).

We now modify (31) to (43), adding Case-marking alongside θ-government:

(43)
α properly governs β iff α θ-governs, Case-marks, or antecedent-governs β.

In terms of (43), it follows that *consider* properly governs t in (40) but not in (41), as required, since it Case-marks t in (40) but not in (41).

Example (22d) poses a problem for the extension of L-marking to include Case-marking:

(22)
d. *how did Bill wonder [$_{CP}$ who wanted [t' [to fix the car t]]]

Recall that *want* does not properly govern t'; if it did, the sentence would be grammatical. It would therefore be necessary to ensure that *want* not Case-mark t' in this instance even though *want* is a Case assigner and governs t', the specifier of the most deeply embedded clause.

Summarizing, it may be possible, though it is not necessary on our assumptions, to extend the definition of "proper government" to include Case-marking as well as direct θ-marking. I will assume that this extension of proper government is not required, keeping the definition in the form (31) and relying on the method of VP-adjunction.

The second question that arises concerning Case-marking involves the consequences for the determination of BCs and barriers if L-marking is extended to include Case-marking alongside θ-government. This affects the definition (25) of "blocking category":

(25)
γ is a BC for β iff γ is not L-marked and γ dominates β.

The extension of L-marking yields different results for an NP that is Case-marked but not θ-marked by V, that is, for Exceptional Case-marking constructions such as (44) as contrasted with (45):

(44)

a. John V [$_\alpha$ NP α]
b. John V [$_{IP}$ NP to VP]

(45)

John V [$_{CP}$ e [$_{IP}$ NP to VP]]

In (44a) and (44b) NP is L-marked and therefore is not a BC, if L-marking includes Case-marking; but in (45) NP is not L-marked and therefore is a BC. It follows that NP in (44) should have essentially the status of an object of the matrix V with regard to extraction and government of its specifier and head from outside, as contrasted with the NP subject of (45). These seem to be the correct conclusions; I return to the matter briefly in section 12. Let us assume now that in fact the embedded subject in (45) behaves like an object and is therefore L-marked by the matrix verb V.

The conjecture now being investigated is that the L-marking of the embedded subject NP by V in (44) is a consequence of Case-marking. If so, then some care is required in formulating the concepts of Case-marking and government. Recall that "government" is defined in terms of the concept of barrier, and the latter is defined in terms of BC, hence in terms of L-marking, including θ-government and, we are now tentatively assuming, Case-marking. We must, then, ensure that θ-government and Case-marking are not defined in terms of government. We have seen that this is straightforward for θ-government, defined in terms of X-bar properties, but the situation with regard to Case-marking is more complex. The latter relation plainly involves government; the standard assumption is that Case-marking takes place only under government.

One approach would be to define the relevant notions recursively. Thus, α 0-L-marks β only if α and β are sisters, where sisterhood is a concept of X-bar theory. "0-BC" and "0-barrier" are then defined in terms of 0-L-marking as above. Then α L-marks β only if there are no 0-barriers protecting β, and "barrier" is defined in terms of L-marking as above. In case (44a), for example, V and α are sisters, so V 0-L-marks α (θ-marking, in this case). Then α is not a 0-barrier, so V L-marks NP (Case-marking, in this case). Then NP is neither a BC nor a barrier for elements within it, and α does not inherit barrierhood from NP. The same holds for (44b). Consider in contrast (45) or (46):

(46)
they believe [$_{CP}$ that [$_{IP}$[$_{NP}$ pictures of John]] are on sale]

In either case the matrix verb 0-L-marks (θ-marks) its sister, CP, so the latter is not a 0-BC. But CP is a 0-barrier for NP by inheritance from IP, so the matrix verb does not L-mark (Case-mark) the embedded subject even if it has a Case feature to assign.

It might be possible to permit α to assign its Case feature freely, then requiring that the Case relation is established only under government. It would then be necessary to show that other properties "conspire" to ensure that only the right consequences ensue. This is a rather delicate matter, since the range of possibilities is quite complex; I will not pursue it here since a different approach, eliminating reference to Case-marking, seems plausible.

We might eliminate reference to Case-marking from the definition of "barrier," avoiding the problems just sketched while still retaining the conclusion that V L-marks NP in (44), simply by stipulating that if α L-marks β under θ-government, then it L-marks the specifier of β. This move might be motivated by considering the relation between the subject of IP and the AGR element of I, the relation that enters into nominative Case assignment and, under some conceptions, the null subject parameter. Suppose that we extend this relation, which I will refer to as "SPEC-head agreement," to the pair (subject, I) more generally, whether or not AGR is present, though the standard effects will follow only if AGR is present to Case-mark or identify the subject. Let us now assume that SPEC-head agreement is a form of "feature sharing" similar to θ-government—in fact, sharing of the features person, number, gender, Case, etc. (the "ϕ-features" of Chomsky 1981 and other work) when AGR is present, and, let us say, sharing of an abstract ϕ-feature F when AGR is missing. Suppose then that we construe L-marking as follows, revising (28):

(47)
Where α is a lexical category, α L-marks β iff β agrees with the head of γ that is θ-governed by α.

We restrict attention here to SPEC-head agreement and assume that any category α agrees with itself and with its head. The effect is that α L-marks the category β that it θ-governs, and if β = IP, its specifier.[21]

Compare now the cases (44), (45), and (46), repeated here:

(44)

a. John V [$_\alpha$ NP α]

b. John V [$_{IP}$ NP [$_I$ to] VP]

(45)

John V [$_{CP}$ e [$_{IP}$ NP [$_I$ to] VP]]

(46)

they believe [$_{CP}$ that [$_{IP}$[$_{NP}$ pictures of John]] [$_I$ are] on sale]

Putting aside (44a) for the moment, we now assume that SPEC-head agreement holds between the embedded NP and I ($=$ *to, are*). In (44b) IP is θ-governed by V; hence, V L-marks IP, its head I, and its specifier NP. Thus, NP is not a BC and IP does not inherit barrierhood from it, as required. In (45) and (46), in contrast, V does not θ-govern IP, so SPEC-head agreement has no effect. The argument will extend to (44a) on either of two assumptions: that there is indeed an I in small clause constructions[22] or that an "agreement" relation of the relevant sort holds between the subject and head of the small clause, so that L-marking is extended to this case in the manner just described.

Let us assume, then, that barrierhood as well as proper government can be defined in terms that exclude Case-marking, avoiding the technical questions that would result from a decision to generalize L-marking to include Case-marking in the definition of "BC." We will return in section 11 to the NP-movement examples in which no Case is assigned to the embedded subject.

Recall that proper government is a proper subcase of government, requiring θ-government or chain coindexing. Thus, even though we are now assuming the embedded subject in (44) to be governed and L-marked by the matrix verb, it is not properly governed by it. The distinction is crucial; it is required to block "super-raising" as in (34), (41), and for other reasons to which we will turn directly.

Evidence provided by Torrego (1985) suggests a slight further generalization of this approach to barriers. Torrego observes that in Spanish an NP can be extracted from a fronted *wh*-phrase (which we assume to be in the specifier position of CP), as in (48a):

(48)

a.   este es el autor [del que]$_i$ no sabemos [$_{CP}$[$_\alpha$ qué libros t_i] leer]

a'. this is the author [by whom]$_i$ we don't know [what books t_i] to read

Here *del que* is extracted from the fronted *wh*-phrase α. Assuming the Condition on Extraction Domains (CED) proposed by Huang (1982) (to which we will return, reducing it to Subjacency), this extraction should be possible only if α is governed by the matrix verb. We conclude again that the specifier of CP can be governed by a verb governing CP.

A further consequence of these assumptions, as Torrego observes, is that the impossibility of extraction from a subject NP (a CED effect) is overcome by *wh*-movement of the subject, as in (49):

(49)
a. *esta es la autora [de la que]$_i$ [$_{IP}$[varias traducciones t_i] han ganado premios internacionales]
a'. this is the author by whom several translations have won international awards
b. [de que autora]$_i$ no sabes [$_{CP}$[qué traducciones t_i] han ganado premios internacionales]
b'. by what author don't you know what translations have won international awards

If these arguments are essentially correct, then if α governs CP, α governs the specifier of CP. Again, it follows that CP cannot be an *inherent* barrier to government. So far this is straightforward: CP is not a barrier to government of its specifier in this case, since it is θ-governed.

We must, however, ensure that the *wh*-phrase *qué libros t_i* in (48a) is not only governed but also L-marked by the matrix verb *sabemos;* otherwise, it will be a BC for t_i, so that it and (by inheritance) CP will be barriers to government, yielding a Subjacency violation (a CED violation). There must, then, be some process that allows V to L-mark the specifier in a structure such as (50):

(50)
V [$_{CP}$ *wh*-phrase C IP]

The question is a familiar one, which arises in various forms in other work on the topic.[23] We tentatively stipulate, then, that the specifier is L-marked by V in the case of a structure such as (50).

One might try to assimilate this property to other familiar cases such as the *que*-to-*qui* rule in French and the fact that the complementizer *that* acts as a proper governor of the subject in English relative clauses, as in (51), so that "sharing of index" is also apparently required:

(51)

NP [$_{CP}$ O [$_C$ that] IP]

Here O is the empty operator formed by relativization, and, essentially, following Pesetsky 1981, we may assume that its index is transmitted to the complementizer head.

Recall once more (22d):

(22)

d. *how did Bill wonder [$_{CP'}$ who wanted [$_{CP}$ t' e [to fix the car t]]]

Following Lasnik and Saito (1984), we assumed that t' is not properly governed by *want,* so that it becomes the "offending trace" by failure of antecedent government. Hence, although the specifier of CP is L-marked by the θ-governor of CP, it is not properly governed by it.

The stipulation that the θ-governor of CP L-marks its specifier falls under the previous assumptions if we assume that SPEC-head agreement holds in this case as well, with sharing of an abstract ϕ-feature between the specifier of CP and its head just as in the case of the specifier of IP and its head.[24] This SPEC-head agreement relation enters into selection as well, if it proves possible (as seems likely) to dispense with [±WH]-features of the head C of CP and establish selectional relations for verbs such as *wonder* at LF; then the *wh*-phrase in specifier position will satisfy the selectional relation by virtue of its agreement with the head C, selection being regarded uniformly as a head-head relation. The concept of selection, then, will be formulated more or less along the lines of the definition (47) of "L-mark."

Note again that the specifier of CP, although L-marked by the θ-governor α of CP, is not θ-governed (hence, properly governed) by α, just as the NP specifier of IP is L-marked but not θ-governed (hence, properly governed) by the V governor of IP in a CP-deletion construction. This is again a crucial distinction, necessary in this case to block "long *wh*-movement" of adjuncts, as in (22d), the analogue now of "super-raising" as in (34), (41).

We now have the following system. Three relations are relevant to the theory of government: θ-government, SPEC-head agreement in IP and CP (the two nonlexical projections), and chain coindexing. The first two relations enter into L-marking and thus into the determination of BCs and barriers. θ-government and chain coindexing, but not SPEC-head agreement, enter into proper government. θ-government holds under the Sisterhood Condition (possibly qualified as in (35)). It seems that references to Case-marking can be eliminated with respect to proper government in favor of VP-adjunction and with respect to barrierhood in favor of SPEC-head agreement. In terms of L-marking, we define "BC," then "barrier," then "government," as outlined above. Proper government is a subcase of government involving the indexing of chain links or θ-government. In section 11 we will consider a possible reduction of proper government to chain links in a slightly extended sense, eliminating θ-government.

6. Subjacency

Consider again example (36):

(36)
how did [$_{IP}$ you [$_{VP}$ fix the car] t]

Although no problem arises in the case of adjunct movement if the structure represented in (36) is an option, there is a problem for movement of a complement from within VP. This is not a problem of government (since complements are θ-governed, hence properly governed), but rather a problem of subjacency. Our intuitive idea is that movement should become "worse" as more barriers are crossed, the best case being the crossing of zero barriers. The best possible case should be (52):

(52)
who did [$_{IP}$ John [$_{VP}$ see t]]

But here two barriers are crossed—namely, VP and IP (which inherits barrierhood from VP)—so that the sentence should violate the Subjacency Condition. This is surely not the correct result.

   Consider (52) more closely. The associated D-Structure representation is (53):

(53)
[$_{CP}$[$_{NP}$ e] [$_{C'}$ C [$_{IP}$ John [$_{I'}$ I [$_{VP}$ see who]]]]]

There are two cases of movement: movement of I to the head position C, and movement of *who* to the specifier position NP of CP. Thus, (52) is an instance of the verb-second phenomenon, in accord with X-bar theory. The movement of I is unproblematic, crossing only the BC IP, which is not a barrier (see (26b)). But the movement of *who* to the matrix specifier position crosses VP, a barrier since it is not L-marked, and IP, a barrier by inheritance from VP.

Recall however that another option is permitted—namely, successive cyclic movement of *who* to VP, then to the specifier of CP, yielding the structure (54):

(54)
who did [$_{IP}$ John [$_{VP}$ t' [$_{VP}$ see t]]]

As we have seen, nothing bars this process, and examples have been discussed involving LF-movement and proper government. In the structure (54) movement to the position of *t'* does not cross the category VP (though it does cross one segment of VP), and the same is true of movement to the clausal specifier position from the adjoined position occupied by *t'*. Hence, no barriers are crossed, as is required. We will look into the technical details more closely in a moment.

Let us now return to the structure (37):

(37)
how did [$_{IP}$ you [$_{VP}$ fix the car t]]

Suppose that this is in fact the only option available for the adjunct. Then successive cyclic movement through VP yields (55):

(55)
how did [$_{IP}$ you [$_{VP}$ t' [$_{VP}$ fix the car t]]]

We must now assume that *t'* antecedent-governs *t*, hence governs *t*. This will be the case, as discussed earlier, only if we accept the definition of "government" given in (18) in terms of exclusion, rather than the definition given in (14) in terms of domination (inclusion).

This example does not yet force a decision if the option (36) is available, but biclausal examples do force a decision. Consider the sentence (56), assuming now that *t* is outside of VP as in (36):

(56)
how does John [$_{VP'}$ think [$_{CP}$[$_{IP}$ you [$_{VP}$ fixed the car] t]]]

Here CP is the complement of *think* within VP'. The adjunct *how* moves from *t* to the specifier of CP. But now movement in one step to the matrix specifier position is impossible; if movement takes place in one step, the trace *t'* in the specifier position of CP will not be properly governed because VP' is a barrier. Therefore, the next step must be adjunction to VP', forming (57):

(57)
[$_{VP'}$ t^2 [$_{VP'}$ think [$_{CP}$ t' ...

But t^2 must properly govern t', which requires the definition of "government" in terms of exclusion. Recall that all the intermediate traces must be present at LF to properly govern the traces of the adjunct, according to the assumptions of Lasnik and Saito that we have adopted here. Hence, these assumptions lead to the conclusion that "government" must be defined in terms of exclusion, as in (18).

Let us now turn to the problem of defining "subjacency" so as to permit successive cyclic movement with adjunction to VP along the lines of the informal account just sketched. The basic principle of bounding theory is that every link (α_i, α_{i+1}) of a chain $(\alpha_1, ..., \alpha_n)$ must meet the Subjacency Condition:[25]

(58)
If (α_i, α_{i+1}) is a link of a chain, then α_{i+1} is subjacent to α_i.

How then should we formulate the concept of subjacency so as to yield the desired results in the earlier case of (54)?

(54)
who did [$_{IP}$ John [$_{VP}$ t' [$_{VP}$ see t]]]

The relevant notion, again, is exclusion, as defined in (17). We can then define the basic concept of bounding theory in these terms:

(59)
β is n-subjacent to α iff there are fewer than $n+1$ barriers for β that exclude α.

Then in (54) t is 0-subjacent to t': there is no barrier including t and excluding t'. Similarly, t' is 0-subjacent to *who*. Thus, (54) is an instance of the best possible case of movement, as required.

In the condition (58) for chain links, by "subjacent" we mean 1-subjacent: that is, in a well-formed chain with a link (α_i, α_{i+1}), α_{i+1} must be 1-subjacent to α_i, and 0-subjacency yields a still more acceptable structure. It is natural that 1-subjacency should play a special role—that is, that crossing two barriers should yield a considerable decrement in acceptability. This would follow from the assumption that languages do not have counters but do employ the concept of adjacency; 1-subjacency is a form of adjacency, but to specify n-subjacency for higher values of n requires counters.[26]

Let us once again consider (22d):

(22)

d. *how did Bill wonder [$_{CP}$ who wanted [t' [PRO to fix the car t]]]

Although this structure yields an ECP violation, as noted, there is nothing to bar a different structure resulting from successive cyclic movement with adjunction to VP. Thus, *how* could first move from the D-Structure position *t* to *t'*, then adjoin to the VP headed by *want*, then adjoin to the VP headed by *wonder,* and finally move to the specifier position of the matrix CP. The structure would then be (60):

(60)

how did Bill [t³ [wonder [$_{CP}$ who [t² [wanted [t¹ [PRO to fix the car t]]]]]]]

Here *t* is properly governed by t^1 and the latter is properly governed by t^2, so it is no longer the "offending trace" violating the ECP at LF, as in the Lasnik-Saito analysis. But now t^2 is not properly governed by its antecedent t^3, CP being a barrier by inheritance from IP, so we still have an ECP violation, as required. The Lasnik-Saito analysis remains in essence, but with a slight modification concerning the choice of "offending trace."

7. Island Violations

Given this formulation of the Subjacency Condition, let us now briefly consider some standard island violations. Consider first the CED, which includes the Subject Condition and the Adjunct Condition, as illustrated in (61) (see also (49a)) and (62), respectively:

(61)

a. the man who [$_{IP}$[pictures of t] are on the table]

b. the book that [$_{IP}$[reading t] would be fun]

(62)

a. to whom did [$_{IP}$ they leave [before speaking t]]

b. who did [$_{IP}$ they leave [before speaking to t]] (before meeting t)

In (61) the embedded subject is not L-marked and is therefore a BC and a barrier. Furthermore, IP inherits barrierhood. Therefore, two barriers are crossed and the sentence violates Subjacency. In (62) the adjunct is a BC and a barrier, and IP again inherits barrierhood. Thus, the CED cases are accommodated directly.

A few comments are in order about this analysis of the CED. First, note that we must assume that *wh*-phrases may not adjoin to IP, then moving to the specifier of CP; thus, we must adopt the stronger of the two options with regard to *wh*-movement (see section 2). There are also empirical questions. Adriana Belletti has pointed out that (62b) is a less severe violation than (62a), a distinction that some speakers find clearer in the corresponding relatives:[27]

(63)
a. he is the person to whom [$_{IP}$ they left [before speaking t]]
b. he is the person who [$_{IP}$ they left [before speaking to t]] (before meeting t)

I will return to this question. As for (61), Kuno (1972) observes that *wh*-movement may be more acceptable with pied-piping, particularly in relatives, which (for unclear reasons) seem to involve less severe violations in some instances, as in (64):

(64)
he is the person of whom [$_{IP}$ pictures are on the table]

A possibility that might be explored is that PP-extraposition can precede *wh*-movement, thus yielding a difference between (64) and cases such as (61a–b), though this raises other questions (see also (49)). I will put these matters aside here, merely noting a potential problem.

The adjunct island case of the CED will yield an ECP violation, typically stronger than a Subjacency violation, in the case of adjunct extraction from an adjunct, as in (65):

(65)
a. *how did you leave [before fixing the car t]
b. *who left [before fixing the car how]
c. who left [before fixing what]

(65a) exhibits both a Subjacency and an overriding ECP violation, and as expected the interpretation is rigidly excluded. In (65b) LF-movement of *how* will also yield an ECP violation. This case contrasts with (65c), where *what* is internally properly governed and therefore can move to the matrix position occupied by *who,* not observing Subjacency, in accord with the assumptions of Huang (1982) and Lasnik and Saito (1984), which we are adopting here, concerning LF-movement. Similarly, analogues in which *John* replaces *who* would yield a grammatical question in (65c) but not (65b) in languages such as Chinese or Japanese that restrict *wh*-movement to LF.

The differences between extraction of adjunct and extraction of argument from an adjunct (a non-θ-governed category) are also illustrated in such constructions as (66a–d):

(66)
a. it [$_{VP}$ is time [$_{CP}$ (for John) to visit Mary]]
b. it [$_{VP}$ is time [$_{CP}$ (for John) to fix the car [that way]]]
c. who is it time (for John) to visit t
d. *how is it time (for John) to fix the car t

In (66a) a *wh*-phrase in the position of *Mary* can first move to the specifier position in CP, then adjoin to VP, and finally move to the specifier position of the matrix clause, yielding (66c), crossing only the barrier CP. The same derivation in the case of (66b), however, with *how* in place of *that way,* yields an ECP violation since the CP barrier blocks antecedent government.

The adjunct island case of the CED is also illustrated by such examples as (67):

(67)
they were too angry to hold the meeting

This is in fact ambiguous, as we can see by replacing *they* first by *the organizers* and then by *the crowds;* in the former case the natural interpretation is that the organizers were so angry that they (the organizers) would not hold the meeting; in the latter case the natural interpretation is that the crowds were so angry that the organizers (not the crowds) could not hold the meeting. The ambiguity is resolved by *wh*-movement. Thus, (68) means only that they were so angry that they (the same group) would not hold the meeting:

(68)
which meeting were they too angry to hold

Such facts would be explained if the two structures corresponding to (67) were something like (69a–b):[28]

(69)
a. [they were [too angry [$_{CP}$ PRO to hold the meeting]]]
b. [$_{IP}$[they were too angry] [$_{CP}$ PRO to hold the meeting]]

In (69a) PRO is c-commanded and hence controlled by *they,* but in (69b) it is not c-commanded by *they* and hence is arbitrary in interpretation. In (69b) CP is ungoverned and hence is a BC and a barrier. Barrierhood is inherited by the matrix IP so that there is a Subjacency violation, an adjunct island violation falling under the CED. In (69a) CP is presumably governed and hence is not a BC, so the *wh*-chain has only 0-subjacency links. If CP is ungoverned, the *wh*-phrase would have one 1-subjacency link, assuming adjunction to AP. Questions arise about how to make these ideas precise, but they seem generally plausible.

If this line of argument is basically correct, then the CED reduces to Subjacency. This seems a plausible conclusion. These effects share the weaker and more variable character of Subjacency violations, as compared with the more rigid government (ECP) violations; moreover, they are S-Structure effects, like other Subjacency violations, which, we assume (following Huang 1982), do not arise in LF-movement.[29]

Let us next consider the Complex Noun Phrase Condition (CNPC). As is well known, a number of factors (including lexical choice) appear to enter into acceptability judgments in these cases, many of them poorly understood. But it seems that a substantial subpart of the phenomena involved can be factored out and assigned to the category of Subjacency violations. These fall into two general categories: relative clause constructions and noun-complement constructions. Typical examples of the former are (70a–d), where *t* is the trace of the matrix *wh*-phrase:

(70)
a. which book did John meet [$_{NP}$ a child [$_{CP}$ who read t]]
b. which book did John have [$_{NP}$ a friend [$_{CP}$ to whom to read t]]
c. to which children did John write [$_{NP}$ a book [$_{CP}$ (for parents) to read t]]
d. which children did John write [$_{NP}$ a book [$_{CP}$ (for parents) to read to t]]

Here the relative clause CP is a BC and a barrier, and the NP, though not a BC because it is θ-governed, inherits barrierhood from CP. Thus, two barriers are crossed, and a Subjacency violation results. Furthermore, *wh*-movement of an adjunct produces a much more extreme ECP violation, as expected:

(71)

how did John meet [$_{NP}$ a man [$_{CP}$ who fixed the car t]]

The noun-complement case of the CNPC typically provides a weaker island effect:

(72)

a. which book did John hear [$_{NP}$ a rumor [$_{CP}$ that you had read t]]
b. which book did John announce [$_{NP}$ a plan [$_{CP}$ (for you) to.read t]]
c. which actor did you see [$_{NP}$ a picture of t]

According to our analysis so far, there are no barriers in these constructions: CP is L-marked; hence, it is not a BC[30] and does not transfer barrierhood to the complex NP, which is also not a BC since it is L-marked.

The "intermediate" status of many such constructions suggests that there is nevertheless one barrier, and this conclusion is reinforced by noting that adjunct extraction is generally impossible, as Lasnik and Saito observe:

(73)

how did John announce [$_{NP}$ a plan [$_{CP}$ to fix the car t]]

This sentence cannot be interpreted as indicated, but only with *how* associated with the matrix verb. It contrasts with (74), where the interpretation analogous to (73) is allowed:

(74)

how did John tell you [to fix the car t]

In (74) successive cyclic movement will provide a chain with antecedent government for each link, so there is no ECP violation (and no Subjacency violation). In (73) the structure provided by successive cyclic movement will be (75):

(75)

how did John announce [$_{NP}$ a plan [$_{CP}$ t^2 to [t^1 fix the car t]]]

Here t and t^1 are antecedent-governed as before, so it must be that t^2 is the offending trace, yielding an ECP violation.

It follows from these considerations that either CP or NP is a barrier to movement, but not both; otherwise, the Subjacency violation will be "too strong." It also follows that CP or NP or perhaps both are barriers to government. The Minimality Condition, to which we will turn in the next section, entails that NP is a barrier to government of t^2, though not a barrier for movement since this condition pertains only to government (see section 4). Therefore, CP must be a barrier to movement (hence, to government), though one that does not transmit barrierhood to NP.

That CP may be a barrier to government is suggested by the fact that the complementizer cannot be deleted in such sentences as (76), implying that the position is not properly governed, if Stowell's theory is correct (see section 4):

(76)
John expressed [NP the feeling [CP *(that) the meeting should not be held]]

Thus, either CP is a barrier to government here or the N head of NP is not a proper governor, a possibility to which we will turn in section 11.

Suppose that CP is indeed a barrier in these constructions. There are several reasons why this might be so. It may be that nouns assign oblique Case and that this imposes an inherent barrier to government.[31] If so, then we will have a typically weak Subjacency violation in a complex noun phrase of the second (noun-complement) type, along with an absolute prohibition against adjunct extraction (and, perhaps, complementizer deletion), by virtue of the ECP.

Consider next the category of Wh-Island Condition violations, with such typical examples as (77a–d):

(77)
a. what$_i$ did you wonder [CP[to whom]$_j$ John gave t$_i$ t$_j$]
b. [to whom]$_j$ did you wonder [what$_i$ John gave t$_i$ t$_j$]
c. what$_i$ did you wonder [CP[to whom]$_j$ to give t$_i$ t$_j$]
d. [to whom]$_j$ did you wonder [what$_i$ to give t$_i$ t$_j$]

In (77a) *what* moves from the position of t_i, adjoining to the lower VP. Still assuming that adjunction to IP is barred for *wh*-movement, the next step is movement to the matrix VP, crossing CP, which inherits barrierhood from the non-L-marked IP. Therefore, one barrier is crossed and a weak Subjacency violation results. The same is true in the other cases. Since one barrier is involved, adjunct movement will always be impossible, by the ECP. Thus, we have such cases as (78a–b), where *how* cannot be associated with the lower verb, as contrasted with such cases as (74), repeated here:

(78)

a. how did John tell you [when to fix the car t]
b. how did John know [which car to fix t]

(74)

how did John tell you [to fix the car t]

These conclusions are acceptable as a first approximation, but some refinement is in order. There appear to be some other relevant factors and perhaps some parametric variation with regard to the *wh*-island effect, probably minor and variable among speakers and languages (see Rizzi 1982, Sportiche 1981). These effects appear to involve the non-lexical categories IP, CP—that is, the clausal system, the nonlexical projections. One relevant factor is tense. Thus, for many speakers (77a–b) are less acceptable than (77c–d), and with nonargument *wh*-phrases the examples perhaps improve further, as in (79) (compare (78)):[32]

(79)

a. which car did John tell you [how to fix t]
b. which car did he wonder [whether to fix]

Suppose, then, that tensed IP is an inherent barrier (possibly weak) to *wh*-movement, over and above the system just outlined, this effect being restricted to the most deeply embedded tensed IP. Then examples (77a–b) will involve the crossing of a second barrier beyond CP, yielding degraded sentences. This assumption yields the major facts that have been discussed concerning such languages as English and French, at least in terms of judgments of relative acceptability.

Rizzi's work suggests a further parametric difference between English and Italian, though in the English case, at least, there seems to be considerable variation among speakers, many of whom accord fairly closely with Rizzi's Italian judgments; this should not be surprising with regard to low-level parametric variation that receives little support in evidence available to the language learner. Suppose that the parameter involved in Rizzi's material relates to the choice of IP vs. CP: that is, in the variety of English under consideration the "extra barrier" is tensed IP, and in Italian it is tensed CP. In both cases we restrict the parameter to the most deeply embedded tensed clause. Choice of tensed CP rather than tensed IP as the value of the parameter adds no barrier in (77), since the lowest CP is already a barrier by inheritance.

This yields the reported difference between Italian and English-French, in such cases as these.

Consider such examples as (80):

(80)

what did you wonder [$_{CP'}$ who [$_{VP'}$ knew [$_{CP}$ who [$_{VP}$ saw t]]]]

As Rizzi notes, these "double *Wh*-Island violations" are more degraded than the case of crossing of a single *wh*-phrase in pre-IP position. In our analysis (80) can be formed by successive cyclic movement, from *t*, to VP, then to VP', then to the matrix VP *wonder CP'*, and finally to the matrix specifier. There are two links of the chain that cross a single barrier. The lessened acceptability suggests that the violations are cumulative. Note that when tensed IP is considered an extra barrier, as above, two barriers are crossed in moving out of the most deeply embedded clause. Furthermore, if violations are cumulative, then the parameter must be restricted to the most deeply embedded tensed clause, as above; otherwise, such sentences as (81) will be severe violations, which is untrue:

(81)

who did you think that John said that Bill saw

Consider finally such sentences as (82a–b):

(82)

a. what did you wonder [$_{CP'}$ who [$_{VP'}$ said [$_{CP}$ that Bill [$_{VP}$ saw t]]]]
b. what did you wonder [$_{CP'}$ who [$_{VP'}$ decided [$_{CP}$ to [$_{VP}$ see t]]]]

Suppose that we take the "Italian value" of the parameter, with the lowest tensed CP adding a barrier. Consider (82a). The *wh*-phrase moves from *t* to VP, then to the specifier position of CP, crossing no barriers. Movement to VP' then crosses one barrier, since tensed CP is a barrier. Further movement to the matrix verb phrase adds a second violation, yielding the equivalent of (80), though there is only one *wh*-island. Suppose now that we take the "English value" of the parameter, with the lowest tensed IP adding a barrier. Then movement from VP to the specifier of CP crosses one barrier and further movement adds a second, yielding the same result as with the "Italian value." In the case of (82a), then, the two choices give the same results, though they differ in the case of (77a–b). Consider next (82b). Movement as far as VP′ crosses no barriers. With the "Italian value," one barrier is crossed (namely, CP′) in the next move, to the matrix clause. With the "English value," however, movement from VP′ to the matrix clause crosses two barriers (namely, CP′ and the medial IP, which is the lowest tensed IP). Again these results conform fairly closely to reported variation in judgment.

Note that the parametric variation is restricted to subjacency, not government, so the "extra barriers" have no effect on adjunct movement. It may be that the parametric variation involves not the distinction tense vs. infinitive but the distinction indicative vs. infinitive-subjunctive, or perhaps some factor involving nonrealized subject. Alternative decisions lead to slightly different conclusions regarding such cases. It seems that the major properties of *wh*-movement as discussed by Rizzi and others can be accommodated in terms of factors involving the clausal system CP, IP, with certain low-level parameters, though various questions remain.

I have omitted here another case of *Wh*-Island Condition violation that arises only in a preposition-stranding language such as English, as in (83):

(83)
who$_i$ did you wonder [$_{CP}$ what$_j$ John [$_{VP}$ gave t$_j$ to t$_i$]]

As is well known, these violations are much more severe than such examples as (77a–d), suggesting that some different factor is involved. One possibility is a version of the earliest proposal concerning these structures, namely, that double application of a rule to a given phrase is barred (see Chomsky 1964). This might follow, on our assumptions, from a condition barring double adjunction of NP to VP, so that (83) would be a much more severe violation of Subjacency. In any event, (83) is barred by considerations apart from the *Wh*-Island Condition, whereas the examples of (77), such as (84) (= (77b)), would be only weak Subjacency violations:

(84)
[to whom]$_i$ did you wonder [$_{CP}$ what$_j$ John [$_{VP}$ gave t$_j$ t$_i$]]

As observed by Kyle Johnson, the discussion can be extended to the theory proposed by Larson (1983) concerning such examples as (85a–c):

(85)

a. I saw Mary in New York [before [she claimed [$_{CP}$ that she would arrive]]]

b. I saw Mary in New York [before [she made [the claim [$_{CP}$ that she had arrived]]]]

c. I saw Mary in New York [before [she asked [$_{CP}$ how to fix the car]]]

Larson observes (following Michael Geis) that (85a) is ambiguous: it may mean that I saw Mary before she made the claim or before the time of her predicted arrival. But the latter interpretation is barred in (85b) and correspondingly in (85c). Larson argues that a temporal *wh*-phrase moves to the pre-IP position of the clausal complement of *before*, violating Subjacency in (85b) and (85c) under the second interpretation, with the temporal phrase within CP. The severity of the violation and the fact that it carries over to weak Subjacency violations such as (85c) suggests, however, that this is an ECP effect, as in the case of adjunct extraction.[33]

In general, these comments carry over to familiar examples of empty operator movement, as in (86), with no further discussion (see Chomsky 1981, 1985):

(86)

a.   John is too stubborn [to talk to]

b.   John is too stubborn [to expect [anyone to talk to]]

c.   *John is too stubborn [to visit [anyone who talked to]]

d.   *John is too stubborn [to ask anyone [who talked to]]

Finally, let us consider rightward movement, which also appears to observe a locality condition akin to Subjacency, the "Right Roof Constraint" proposed by Ross (1967). Consider (87), where either t or t' appears but not both:

(87)

[$_{NP}$ many books [$_{PP}$ with [stories t]] t']] were sold [$_{CP}$ that I wanted to read]

Here CP may have moved from t' but not from t. Movement from t would cross the barriers PP and (by inheritance) NP, yielding a Subjacency violation. Movement from t' satisfies Subjacency, assuming that CP is adjoined to VP or IP. Only the latter choice is possible unless extraposition is a rule of the PF component, not feeding VP-fronting, since the extraposed clause does not move with the VP in this case.

That the rule may indeed be in the PF component has often been proposed in one form or another (for example, by considering it a "post-
cyclic rule" in earlier works such as Ross 1967); it is suggested by the
question of proper government of the trace, which will not arise under
this proposal if the ECP is an LF phenomenon.[34] Further evidence to
this effect is provided by Ross (1983), who observes that binding of an
anaphor is possible with extraposition in such structures as (88a–b):

(88)
a. they desired [that [pictures t] be painted of each other]
b. they desired [that [stories t] be told about each other]

If these structures enter the LF component, one would expect a binding theory violation (Specified Subject Condition). Taraldsen (1981) observes that extraposition modifies possibilities of pronominal binding;
however, this does not suffice to show that the rule produces structures
that enter the LF component, since the relevant properties do not appear to be expressible in terms of the LF binding theory in any event.
Note that extraposition structures such as (87) cannot be considered
predication structures, since they include PP-extraposition (as in (88) or
a picture arrived of John) and complement-extraposition (*the statement
was made that IP*).

   There is also good evidence that the Subjacency Condition holds
only for movement rules, not for similar constructions that cannot involve movement; see Chomsky 1981.

   A problem for this approach, noted by Howard Lasnik (personal
communication), is posed by such structures as (89):

(89)
[$_{NP}$ many proofs [$_{PP}$ of [the theorem t]] t'] appeared [$_{CP}$ that I wanted to
think about]

As in (87), extraposition of CP is possible from t' but not from t. But in
this case, as distinct from (87), PP is not a barrier since it is the complement of *proof*, so NP does not inherit barrierhood. Even if we assume, as above, that oblique Case adds a barrier, still only one barrier
will be crossed by extraposition from t though this clearly should count
as a Subjacency violation, assuming the preceding discussion. A possibility that might be explored is that extraposition is indeed a PF rule
and that θ-government does not play the role in determining barriers in
the PF component that it does in the syntactic and LF components.

This discussion covers the main island effects concerning "move-ment to COMP" and a number of ECP cases as well.

---

8. The Minimality Condition

So far we have restricted attention to the first concept of barrier, namely (15). Let us now turn to the second concept, the "Minimality Condition," which holds of the configuration (19):

(15)
$$\ldots\alpha\ldots[_\gamma \ldots\beta\ldots]$$

(19)
$$\ldots\alpha\ldots[_\gamma \ldots\delta\ldots\beta\ldots]$$

Let us formulate the condition as follows:

(90)
α does not govern β in (19) if γ is a projection of δ excluding α.

Thus, δ "protects" β from government by α even though γ may not be a barrier or even a maximal projection.

A narrower formulation of the Minimality Condition adds the re-quirement (91):

(91)
γ immediately dominates β.

We thus extend the concept of barrier defined earlier to include the following case, for the theory of government but not the theory of movement:

(92)
γ is a barrier for β if γ is (a projection, the immediate projection) of δ, a zero-level category distinct from β.

Choice of "the immediate projection" in (92) gives the narrower con-cept including (91); choice of "a projection" gives the broader concept. Given γ, β as in (92), a category α excluded by γ will not govern β.

The two formulations have different consequences with regard to government of the specifier of γ from outside of γ. This is permitted under the narrow formulation (91) but would be blocked under (90), as in (93), where *picture* governs *Bill:*

(93)

they saw [$_{NP}$ Bill's [$_{N'}$ picture of Tom]]

One consequence of the Minimality Condition, under either formulation, is that in (93) *see* does not govern *Tom*. This seems appropriate, though it is not easy to find empirical consequences of the decision in this case. Thus, suppose that *see* governs *Tom* in the underlying structure (94), prior to *of*-insertion:[35]

(94)

[$_{N'}$ picture Tom]

There are four major consequences to government: the ECP, Case-marking, θ-marking, and L-marking, with its implications for barrier-hood. No issue can arise concerning the ECP, since *picture* already properly governs its complement. Nor can a problem arise concerning Case-marking; if *see* assigns its Case to *Tom,* then the NP *Bill's picture of Tom* will lack Case, violating the Case Filter.[36] The same consideration blocks θ-marking of *Tom* by *see,* though this would also be barred by the Sisterhood Condition (24) on θ-marking. Considerations of L-marking and barrierhood also do not arise, since *Tom* is already L-marked independently of *see,* and *see* does not θ-govern *Tom.*

Despite the lack of obvious empirical consequences in this case, let us assume the Minimality Condition, thus preventing government of *Tom* by *see* in (93). This seems natural on conceptual grounds: it means that the complement of a head cannot be governed by a more remote head.

Another consequence of the Minimality Condition, again under either formulation, is that independently of choice of barriers as defined in terms of BCs, government of t^2 is blocked in (95) (= (75)), yielding an ECP violation as required; thus, *plan* protects t^2 from government in this case:

(95)

how did John announce [$_{NP}$ a plan [$_{CP}$ t^2 to [t^1 fix the car t]]]

It follows that even if no barriers to movement are assumed to exist in the noun-complement constructions, still adjuncts will not be extractable from this kind of complex noun phrase.

Note that the narrower Minimality Condition including (91) goes only part way toward guaranteeing uniqueness of government; thus, in accordance with (91), though *see* does not govern the complement of *picture* in (93), it does govern its specifier, *Bill,* which is outside of N', although *Bill* is also governed by *picture*.[37] The broader Minimality Condition (90) would prevent government of the specifier *Bill* by *see* in this case, thus guaranteeing uniqueness of government by a lexical head. Let us consider the choice between these alternatives.

For reasons discussed earlier, we have been assuming that the specifier of α is governable from outside, where α is CP or infinitival; this would be possible under (90) only if the heads C and I of CP and IP, respectively, are not possible choices for δ in (19). On the other hand, if we adopt the narrower condition (91), it follows that specifiers and heads can be uniformly governed from outside but complements cannot be.

In the case of structures such as (93), there can be no consequences to the choice between the broader and narrower formulations with regard to θ-marking, Case-marking, and L-marking, for the reasons just given, apart from the considerations of note 36. The only consequences, then, relate to the ECP. The relation of *see* to *Bill* in (93) is irrelevant in this connection, because even if *see* governs *Bill,* it does not θ-govern it and therefore cannot properly govern it.

It seems that the major empirical consequences to adopting the Minimality Condition in the narrower form (91) will relate to antecedent government, as in structures of the form (96), where t is the subject of NP:

(96)
wh- $[_{IP} ...[_{VP} V [_{NP} ...t...]]]$

In this structure t is antecedent-governed under the narrower Minimality Condition, though not under the broader Minimality Condition. Thus, choice of the narrower Minimality Condition has a direct empirical consequence: it permits *wh*-movement of the subject of an NP, which is blocked by the broader Minimality Condition since the trace would not be properly governed.

In fact, the consequences are a bit sharper. Under the narrower Minimality Condition, *wh*-extraction of a subject can occur as in (96) but cannot take place over a *wh*-island, which would block antecedent government.

These consequences of the narrower Minimality Condition (91) cannot be tested directly for phrases of the form (93), because extraction of the subject *Bill* is barred for other reasons, presumably having to do with Case theory. But *wh*-movement of the subject of an NP is possible in the Romance languages (for discussion, see Cinque 1980). Torrego

(1985) argues that in Spanish subject-extraction is in fact blocked by a *wh*-island, as illustrated by such examples as (97a–c):

(97)

a. [de qué pintor]$_i$ me has dicho que van a exponer varios dibujos t$_i$
a'. by which painter did you tell me that they are going to exhibit several drawings
b. [de qué pintor]$_i$ me preguntaste si van a exponer varios dibujos t$_i$
b'. by which painter did you ask me whether they are going to exhibit several drawings
c. [de cual de estas ediciones]$_i$ no sabes si hay traducción francesa t$_i$
c'. of which of these editions don't you know whether there is a French translation

Examples (97a) and (97c) are acceptable, but (97b) is deviant; the same distinction seems relatively clear in English despite the marked character of the constructions. In (97c) the *wh*-phrase is the complement of the noun *traducción* and therefore is properly governed internally to the NP, so it can be extracted with at most a weak *wh*-island effect; in (97b), however, the subject is not internally properly governed, and antecedent government is blocked by the *wh*-island, yielding an ECP violation. The distinction between (97b) and (97c) indicates that (97b) is not simply a Subjacency violation. Example (97a) is a standard example of successive cyclic movement.

If this line of argument is correct, we have additional evidence that NP is not an absolute barrier to government and that in general the specifier of a construction can be governed from outside it. We also have evidence for the narrower Minimality Condition (91).

Let us take a closer look at just why the structure (97b) would be an ECP violation under the set of assumptions we are now considering, using the English case for illustration:

(97)

b'. by which painter did you [$_{VP'}$ ask me [$_{CP}$ whether they are going to [$_{VP}$ exhibit [several drawings t]]]]

The *wh*-phrase first moves from *t* to VP. Since *wh*-extraction of the subject is permitted and the subject is not internally properly governed, it must be that *t* is antecedent-governed in the resulting structure (98):

(98)

[$_{VP}$ *wh*- [$_{VP}$ exhibit [several drawings t]]]

This will follow only if we adopt the definition of "government" in terms of exclusion, as in (18). Recall that this will permit *wh*-movement of adjuncts such as *how, why* even if they are within VP. See the discussion of (55), (56), (57).

The *wh*-phrase next moves from its position in (98) across the *wh*-island in (97c), yielding (99):

(99)

[$_{VP'}$ *wh*- [$_{VP'}$ ask me [$_{CP}$ whether they are going to [$_{VP}$ t' [$_{VP}$ exhibit [several drawings t]]]]]]

It must be that *t'* is the offending trace, yielding an ECP violation. Still assuming the framework of Lasnik and Saito (1984), *t'* must be present at LF with the feature $[-\gamma]$. The trace will indeed be assigned this feature since it is not properly governed, but *t'* must not be permitted to delete in the LF component or there will be no ECP violation. The case would therefore be analogous to (22d):

(22)

d. how did Bill [t^3 [wonder [$_{CP}$ who [t^2 [wanted [t^1 [to fix the car t]]]]]]]

Lasnik and Saito argue that for adjuncts γ-assignment takes place at LF, whereas for arguments it takes place at S-Structure. Hence, on the assumptions we are now examining, the subject of an NP must be regarded as falling in the category of adjuncts, not arguments, with regard to the ECP. This is not unreasonable. The intuitive motivation that Lasnik and Saito suggest for the distinction in the treatment of arguments and adjuncts, which remains to be made precise, is in terms of the Projection Principle: arguments are necessary at S-Structure but adjuncts are not. Pursuing the intuition, we might assimilate "Subject of NP" to adjuncts, in that these elements are not in the domain of the Projection Principle and can in fact be missing freely. Subjects of clauses are crucially different; by the Extended Projection Principle, they must be present at S-Structure. Hence, they must be subjected to the ECP (receive γ-marking) at S-Structure.

The preceding discussion shows that a variety of consequences flow from the assumption that subjects of noun phrases can in principle be extracted by *wh*-movement but not over a *wh*-island. Unfortunately, the relevant facts do not appear to be very sharp. Further empirical evidence is required, but the logic of the situation is rather clear.[38]

Let us consider further the narrower version of the Minimality Condition, assuming that in (19) α does not govern β, which is protected by the projection γ of its governor δ. Then in (93) *see* governs *Bill* but not *Tom,* just as a verb governs the specifier of its clausal complement:

(19)

...α...[$_\gamma$ ...δ...β...]

(93)

they saw [$_{NP}$ Bill's [$_{N'}$ picture of Tom]]

This assumption once again has certain consequences for antecedent government in adjunction structures. Consider the following example, discussed earlier:

(100)

how do you [t^2 [want [t^1 [PRO to fix the car t]]]]

Recall that t^1 is antecedent-governed by t^2 and is governed, but not properly governed, by *want*. The relevant part of the structure is (101):

(101)

[$_{VP}$ t^2 [$_{VP}$ ([$_{V'}$) want [$_{CP}$ t^1...

The bracket placed in parentheses is permitted by X-bar theory but, we have assumed, is not required when the specifier is missing; see (3). If the bracket labeled V' appears, then the Minimality Condition will prevent t^2 from governing t^1. Therefore, the Minimality Condition requires that we adopt the convention assumed earlier (see (3b)): bar (prime) structure need not be present when not required. Note that the closer governor *want* does not prevent t^2 from governing t^1 if the parenthesized bracket labeled V' is missing, because t^2 is not excluded by VP.

The Minimality Condition might be invoked to yield the *that*-trace effect, as in (102):

(102)

a.   who did you believe [$_{CP}$ t' [$_{C'}$ e [$_{IP}$ t would win]]]
b.   *who did you believe [$_{CP}$ t' [$_{C'}$ that [$_{IP}$ t would win]]]

In (102b) t is protected from antecedent government by C (= *that*), by virtue of the Minimality Condition, but in (102a) this will not be the case if we make the natural assumption that *e* is featureless[39] and therefore does not serve as an appropriate choice for δ in (19); the intuition is that a minimal governor must be a category with features to serve as a barrier to government. There are various ways to make this precise, and it is difficult to see what evidence might choose among them; for concreteness, let us suppose that X′ is present only when its head has features, so that C′ is missing at D-Structure in (102a), hence throughout the derivation. In this way, the *that*-trace effect is reduced to an ECP violation.

The Minimality Condition as just formulated has an unwanted consequence in the case of successive cyclic movement of an adjunct, yielding at LF a representation including (103), where $t′$ must antecedent-govern t (see (55)–(57)):

(103)
$[_{CP}$ t′ $[_{IP}$ NP $[_{I′}$ I $[_{VP}$ t $[_{VP}$ ...]]]]]

Apart from the Minimality Condition, there are no barriers to government of t by $t′$, because of the defective character of IP; see (26b). But according to the Minimality Condition, I′ will constitute a barrier. Therefore, we must assume that the defective character of the I-system includes both projections: IP and I′.

---

9. Vacuous Movement

So far I have been assuming that a language may have either syntactic *wh*-movement (English), LF *wh*-movement (Chinese, Japanese), or both (French). Considerations of language acquisition suggest another possible option. Suppose the data consist of examples of the following sort:

(104)
a. who likes John
b. who does John like

Example (104b) indicates that syntactic *wh*-movement is permitted, but (104a) is consistent with the assumption that it does not take place. A conclusion consistent with the evidence would be that *wh*-movement takes place except for subjects—that is, the case of "vacuous movement." This proposal is developed by George (1980). If we adopt it, then there are a variety of consequences; for example, *wh*-island effects will be removed for embedded *wh*-subjects, as in (105):

(105)
what do you wonder $[_{CP}$ who saw t]

Here *what* can move from its D-Structure position *t* to the specifier of the embedded CP, which is not occupied by *who,* and then to the matrix specifier position.

Whatever the merits of this proposal may be, there is still good reason to suppose that at LF *who* has moved to the pre-IP position of the embedded clause of (105). Considerations of selection, scope, and absorption (in the sense of Higginbotham and May 1981) strongly support this conclusion.

The same conclusion also follows from consideration of adjunct movement. Compare the examples (106a) and (106b):

(106)
a.   who knows how John did what
b. *who knows what John did how

We have not yet worked out the specific mechanisms of LF-movement of *wh*-in-situ, but it is clear from (106) that they must have the property that the *wh*-phrase fronted at LF occupies a position in which it does not govern its trace; thus, (106b), which requires proper government of the trace of *how* at LF, is barred, whereas (106a), which does not require proper government of the trace of *what* at LF, is grammatical. Now compare (105), which is at worst a weak *Wh*-Island Condition violation, with (107), which is presumably an ECP violation:

(107)
*how do you wonder [$_{CP}$ who fixed the car t]

If *how* were permitted to move through the embedded pre-IP position while *who* remained in situ at LF in (107), then this sentence should be perfectly grammatical, with *t* properly governed by the trace of *how* in the specifier position of the embedded CP. It must therefore be the LF-movement of *who* to the specifier position that yields an ECP violation, either because the trace of *how* is eliminated so that *t* of (107) violates the ECP, or because the raised *who* is unable to properly govern its trace with the trace of *how* present,[40] resulting in a Superiority violation, presumably reducible to the ECP, exactly as in the case of (108):

(108)
*I wonder what who saw

We conclude, then, that the "Vacuous Movement Hypothesis" (VMH) can be adopted only in a slightly different form: vacuous movement is not obligatory at S-Structure. But more general considerations, presumably having to do with questions of scope at LF, require that *wh*-phrases move to the specifier position of CP at LF whenever they remain in situ at S-Structure: multiple *wh*-phrases, Chinese-Japanese type languages, and vacuous movement cases. The rich array of consequences of the latter assumption offers it quite substantial support.

The VMH makes intuitive sense. It would mean that UG requires that *wh*-phrases appear in the position of specifier of CP at LF but that the language learner assumes that there is syntactic movement only where there is overt evidence for it. We might suppose that the unmarked case for a language with overt *wh*-movement is that it always takes place at S-Structure, so that nonmovement of subject in English would have a somewhat marked character, accounting for the persistence of weak island effects even with *wh*-subjects, as in (105).

If the VMH is correct, we should expect to find that in such examples as (109) (due to Luigi Rizzi), the (a)-case should be more acceptable than the (b)-case, with trace indicated only for the relative:

(109)
a. he is the man to whom I wonder [t' [who knew [which book to give t]]]
b. he is the man to whom I wonder [who John told [which book to give t]]

In (109a) *to whom* can move from *t* to *t'* (this position being filled at LF by *who*), but a comparable derivation is blocked in (109b), which would then be a more serious *Wh*-Island Condition violation. The conclusion seems correct, though the facts are hardly crystal clear.

It has often been noted that *whether* yields a much weaker *wh*-island effect than moved *wh*-phrases; thus, (110) is more acceptable than (109b):

(110)
he is the man to whom I wonder [whether John told us [which book to give]]

This would follow if *whether* is base-generated as the head of CP; then in our terms it will move at LF to the specifier position for scopal reasons, eliminating whatever is there. Thus, (110) would be analogous to (109a), involving a kind of vacuous LF-movement. Notice that this assumption would still block adjunct extraction over *whether*, as in (111):

(111)

*how did you know [whether to fix the car t]

Here there will be an ECP violation at LF, as discussed earlier.

The VMH accounts for a variety of phenomena discussed by Chung and McCloskey (1983). The following are typical examples:

(112)

a. this is a paper [that we need to find [someone [$_{CP}$ who understands t]]]

b. this is a paper [that we need to find [someone [$_{CP}$ that we can intimidate with t]]]

c. this is the reason [why we need to find [someone [$_{CP}$ who understands this paper t]]]

d. this is the reason [why we need to find [someone [$_{CP}$ that we can intimidate with this paper t]]]

In (112a) the VMH permits movement of the relative clause operator from t first to the specifier position of CP, then to its final position, yielding only the very weak CNPC effect typical with *someone* as the head of the NP; the trace in the specifier position of CP is then covered by *who* at LF. In (112b) the corresponding derivation is impossible since the specifier position of CP is occupied by the fronted object of *intimidate,* and the expression is less acceptable. Examples (112c) and (112d), corresponding structurally to (112a) and (112b), respectively, are impossible under the given interpretation. In (112c), as in (112a), *why* can move from t first to the specifier position of CP, then to its final position, with only a weak CNPC effect, but an ECP violation results as in (107), since *why* is an adjunct.[41] In (112d) there is a stronger Subjacency violation as in (112b) but also an overriding ECP violation. The full range of facts follows from the VMH.

Chung and McCloskey rely on the Generalized Phrase Structure Grammar assumption that a clause is subjectless if its subject is relativized or questioned. Further elaboration would be required to account for adjunct movement as in (106), (107), (111), (112). As noted, there is good reason to suppose that *wh*-in-situ moves to pre-IP position at LF. The simplest and most natural account appears to be the VMH, which, along with the LF condition on scope, accommodates the full range of relevant phenomena fairly closely with no need for special rule systems or special assumptions regarding subject *wh*-phrases.

Assuming the VMH, UG incorporates the following general principles:

(113)
a. Selectional properties are satisfied under government at LF.
b. Scopal properties require that *wh*-phrases be in pre-IP position at LF.
c. Chain formation can only be initiated from IP-internal positions.

In accordance with (113a), a verb such as *wonder* must govern a *wh*-phrase in the clause it selects, whereas *think* may not. Thus, (114a–c) are grammatical but (114d) is not, whereas in (114e) the embedded subject *who* moves to the matrix specifier position (along with *what*), so that *think* properly selects a declarative clause:

(114)
a. I wonder [$_{CP}$ who [t saw Bill]]
b. I wonder [$_{CP}$ who [Bill saw t]]
c. I wonder [$_{CP}$ who [t saw what]]
d. I thought [who [t saw what]]
e. who thought [$_{CP}$[$_{IP}$ who saw what]]

Principle (113b) requires LF-movement in (114). Principle (113c) permits derivation of the required LF representations by LF-movement, with empirical consequences of the sort just sketched. The restriction to IP-internal positions in (113c) bars the interpretation (115) for (114d), as well as the interpretation (116b) for (116a), with *what* moving to the position of the matrix clause specifier (the interpretation assigned to (116c):[42]

(115)
who did I think saw what

(116)
a. who thinks [what Bill saw]
b. for which person *x* and which thing *y*, *x* thinks that Bill saw *y*
c. who thinks that Bill saw what

The parametric variation distinguishing English from Chinese-Japanese with regard to *wh*-movement could be stated in the following terms:

(117)
At LF, *wh*-phrases move nonvacuously only to a position occupied by *wh*-.

This property does not hold of Chinese-Japanese, but it does hold of English.[43] We may assume further that the negative value for the parameter (117)—the Chinese-Japanese value—entails that there is no syntactic *wh*-movement. With the negative value of the parameter, then, there is no syntactic *wh*-movement at all and a D-Structure *wh*-phrase is permitted to move at LF whether or not the target position is occupied by a *wh*-phrase; furthermore, by general conditions already discussed, *wh*-phrases must move to the specifier of CP at LF. Thus, these languages have *wh*-in-situ for simple interrogatives. In English, in contrast, a *wh*-phrase in situ must move to specifier of CP (by (113b), combined with previous conditions), and it may do so nonvacuously only if this position is already occupied by a *wh*-phrase; *wh*-in-situ is "attracted" by a *wh*-phrase in "scopal" position. This yields the familiar phenomena described originally by Baker (1970) and bars unwanted cases. Thus, consider (118a–f):

(118)
a. who knows [$_{CP'}$ where John remembers [$_{CP}$ that Bill saw what]]
b. you wonder who saw what
c. *you saw what
d. you remember what John saw
e. *you remember that John saw what
f. *you remember that John said who would read what

In (118a) *what* may either have matrix clause scope (associated with *who* by absorption) or have scope over CP' (associated with *where*), but the sentence may not be understood as (119), even though *remember* selects a *wh*-headed proposition:

(119)
who knows where John remembers what Bill saw

In (118b) *what* may have the scope of *who* but not matrix scope, with the meaning "for which *x*, you wonder who saw *x*." Example (118c) has no interpretation (apart from echo-question interpretation, here irrelevant). Example (118d) cannot be understood as the interrogative "what do you remember that John saw?" Example (118e) has no (nonecho) interpretation, nor does (118f). In particular, (118e) cannot mean "you remember what John saw," and (118f) cannot mean either of the following, though these are derivable by *wh*-movement and satisfy selectional properties:

(120)
a. who do you remember that John said would read what
b. you remember who John said would read what

---

10. Parasitic Gaps

Let us turn now to parasitic gaps, and ask how the foregoing considerations relate to the analysis of these constructions, which have provided a good deal of insight into linguistic structure since the topic was opened for investigation by Taraldsen (1981).

One basic property of parasitic gaps is that they are typically licensed by a *wh*-trace (or other operator-bound trace) in object position but not in subject position, as illustrated in (121), where *t* is the real gap and *e* the parasitic gap:[44]

(121)
a.   what did you file t [before reading e]
b.   what did you file t [before you read e]
c.   *who [t met you [before you recognized e]]

The restriction concerning subjects must be qualified, however. A subject can license a parasitic gap that it does not c-command, as noted by Longobardi (forthcoming), who observes that (122b) is more acceptable than (122a):

(122)
a.   *a man who [t looks old [whenever I meet e]]
b.   a man who [whenever I meet e] [t looks old]

Where the subject is more deeply embedded, it can regularly license a parasitic gap, as in the following example due to Andrew Barss (see Engdahl 1983):

(123)
a.   which papers did John decide to tell his secretary t were unavailable before reading e
b.   which papers did John decide [before reading e] to tell his secretary [t' [t were unavailable]]
c.   *which papers [t were unavailable [before you discovered e]]

The position of the *before*-phrase in (123a) is ambiguous, but the ambiguity is resolved in (123b), where the phrase is associated with the matrix clause and the embedded subject *t* licenses the parasitic gap *e;* if the *before*-phrase is construed with the embedded clause in (123a), so that *e* is c-commanded by *t*, the construction is excluded, as in (123c), where *t* c-commands *e*. The exclusion of subject-licensing for parasitic gaps, then, seems to relate to an "anti-c-command" requirement of some sort.

In Chomsky 1982 examples such as (124), with PRO controlled by *you*, are cited as ungrammatical:

(124)
these are the articles that you knew [t were written by Bill] even without [PRO analyzing e]

Preposing the adjunct phrase as in the preceding example gives (125):

(125)
these are the articles that you knew [without analyzing e] [t were written by Bill]

This seems to have about the same status as (123b), which means that (124) should also be acceptable under the intended interpretation. I will put this question aside, along with a number of others concerning factors that enter into acceptability of parasitic gap constructions.

A further property of these constructions is that the parasitic gap shows all of the typical island effects. Consider such examples as (127a–k), assuming them to appear in the context (126):

(126)
this is the man John interviewed t before ____

(127)
a. expecting us to tell you to give the job to e
b. expecting us to ask you which job to give to e
c. asking you which job to give to e
d. wondering who to ask which job to give to e
e. telling you that you should give the job to e
f. reading the book you gave to e
g. hearing about the plan you proposed to e
h. announcing the plan to speak to e
i. hearing about the plan to speak to e
j. expecting you to leave without meeting e
k. meeting the man in the office near e

The relative acceptability of these examples matches that of the corresponding examples with *wh*-movement, such as (128a–b) (corresponding to (127a–b)), etc.:

(128)
a. who did they expect us to tell you to give the job to t
b. who did they expect us to ask you which job to give to t

The matching is in fact quite close; thus, the CNPC cases (127h–i) of the noun-complement type are somewhat more acceptable than the corresponding cases (129f–g) of the relative clause type, and examples such as (127j) are somewhat less extreme violations than many of the others, just as is true of the corresponding cases with *wh*-movement (see (72), (63)).

In short, it seems clear that the parasitic gap construction involves empty operator movement, thus falling into the same category as adjective complements, purposive-rationale clauses, and many others that have been extensively investigated in recent years. In a construction such as (121a), for example, the structure must be something like (129), where O is an empty operator:

(129)
what did you file t [before [O [reading e]]]

This conclusion entails that the analysis in Chomsky 1982 cannot be correct. There it was assumed that the parasitic gap becomes a variable at S-Structure, locally bound by the operator of the real gap and thus falling within its scope. But that cannot be so if the parasitic gap construction involves a chain independent of the chain of the real gap.

It appears, then, that the parasitic gap construction involves an operation of chain composition:

(130)
If $\mathscr{C} = (\alpha_1,\ldots,\alpha_n)$ is the chain of the real gap and $\mathscr{C}' = (\beta_1,\ldots,\beta_m)$ is the chain of the parasitic gap, then the "composed chain"

$$(\mathscr{C},\mathscr{C}') = (\alpha_1,\ldots,\alpha_n,\beta_1,\ldots,\beta_m)$$

is the chain associated with the parasitic gap construction and yields its interpretation.

The question of when parasitic gaps are licensed becomes, then, a question of the conditions under which chain composition is permissible.

Note that this conclusion eliminates much of the motivation for functional determination of empty categories, as discussed in Chomsky 1981, 1982. For additional argument against this approach, see Brody 1984. I have been assuming throughout that the approach is incorrect and that the features assigned to empty categories (like other features) do not change in the course of a derivation; see Chomsky 1985 for further discussion.

In Chomsky 1982 an argument against empty operator movement was suggested, based on examples such as (131a–c):

(131)
a. which book did you file t [without believing [Mary would like e]]
b. which book did you file t [without believing [e would please Mary]]
c. which book did you file t [without believing [that e would please Mary]]

The factual assumption was that (131b) was less acceptable than (131a); then (131b) could be considered an ECP violation, so that it is not formed by movement of an empty category, which would permit e to be properly governed by its antecedent. I noted that the status of (131c), which is considerably less acceptable than (131b), thus remained unexplained. The foregoing considerations suggest that the crucial distinction is between (131b) and (131c), the latter an ECP violation of the *that*-trace variety. What is now unexplained is the difference between (131a) and (131b) (if indeed it is real). These conclusions seem more true to the facts.

We have so far considered one major case of the parasitic gap construction, namely, adjunct parasitic gaps. Turning to the second major case, subject parasitic gaps such as (132), we find that here too there is evidence that parasitic gap constructions involve empty operator movement:

(132)
who would [a picture of e] surprise t

The properties of these parasitic gap constructions are somewhat different from those of the adjunct category, but again it appears that they exhibit the typical island effects. Consider, for example, the following cases:

(133)

a. he's a man that [anyone who talks to e] usually likes t

b. he's a man that [anyone who tells people to talk to e] usually likes

c. *he's a man that [anyone who meets people who talk to e] usually likes

d. *he's a man that [anyone who asks when to talk to e] usually likes

Examples (133a) and (133b) are acceptable; island violations such as (133c) and (133d) are far worse, and the usual range of properties holds, though the examples appear to degrade more rapidly than the adjunct cases. We conclude, then, that this category of parasitic gaps also involves operator movement.

Further insight into the construction is given by such examples as (134a–c):

(134)

a. he's a man that [everyone who [gives presents to e]] likes t

b. *this is a book that [any man to whom [we'll give e]] will like t

c. *he's a man that [any present [they'll give to e]] will please t

Compare *wh*-movement cases that yield phrases identical to those internally bracketed in (134):

(135)

a. he's a man that they wonder who [gives presents to e]

b. this is a book that they wonder [to whom [we'll give e]]

c. *he's a man that they wonder [which presents [they'll give to e]]

Here (135a) and (135b) are typical *Wh*-Island Condition violations, whereas (135c) is a much more severe violation barred by other factors, as we have seen; recall (83). Presumably the same factors explain the status of (134c). Turning to (134a–b), we would expect both to be acceptable—in fact, comparable to (135a–b), which add a *Wh*-Island Condition violation. But although the conclusion is correct with regard to (134a), the unacceptability of (134b) is unexplained.

These examples are quite typical. The examples of subject parasitic gaps that appear in the literature are of the type of (134a), not (134b); structures of the latter type are uniformly unacceptable as parasitic gap constructions.

The correct generalization seems to be that subject parasitic gaps involve the VMH. Examples (134a–b) have the D-Structure representations (136a–b), respectively, where α is the real gap, β is the parasitic gap, and γ is the specifier of CP:

(136)
a. he's a man that [everyone [$_{CP}$ γ [who gives presents to β]]] likes α
b. *this is a book that [any man [$_{CP}$ γ [we'll give β [to whom]]]] will like α

The element α moves to the specifier position of the matrix relative clause, yielding the structures (137a–b), where t is the real gap:

(137)
a. he's a man that [everyone [$_{CP}$ γ [who gives presents to β]]] likes t
b. this is a book that [any man [$_{CP}$ γ [we'll give β [to whom]]]] will like t

By the VMH, *who* may remain in situ at S-Structure in (137a) so that β moves to γ, yielding (138), with e the parasitic gap bound by the empty operator O:

(138)
he's a man that [everyone [$_{CP}$ O [who gives presents to e]]] likes t

But in (137b) the *wh*-phrase *to whom* moves to γ, yielding (139):

(139)
this is a book that [any man [$_{CP}$[to whom]$_i$ [we'll give β t$_i$]]] will like t

Now it is impossible for β to move to the specifier position of CP. We cannot derive a parasitic gap construction with an operator-variable structure, so that (134b) is ungrammatical.

Recall that in (138) *who* must move to the specifier position of CP at LF. Therefore, either parasitic gaps are licensed at S-Structure and O is eliminated by LF-movement, or O vacates its position prior to LF-movement of *who*. There is good evidence that parasitic gaps are licensed at S-Structure; thus, *wh*-in-situ and quantifier phrases do not license parasitic gaps (see Chomsky 1982), so that the chain composition algorithm presumably applies at S-Structure. It also seems reasonable to suppose that the parasitic gap construction must appear at LF for appropriate interpretation, so presumably O does move prior to LF, to a position in which it still locally binds the parasitic gap e. There are several possibilities, but I will not pursue them here; for concreteness, let us assume that O moves to the specifier position of the relative clause, adjoining to the operator binding the real gap.

We conclude that a parasitic gap construction involves two chains $\mathscr{C}$ and $\mathscr{C}'$, where $\mathscr{C}$ is the chain of the real gap and $\mathscr{C}'$ is the chain of the parasitic gap. These are formed into a single chain $(\mathscr{C},\mathscr{C}')$ in accordance with a chain composition condition that is still to be formulated and that must be satisfied at S-Structure. This requirement holds for both adjunct and subject parasitic gap constructions. The VMH holds. Apart from this, no special assumptions are required to derive the array of evidence just reviewed.

The island properties that hold of both types of parasitic gaps provide direct evidence that operator movement is involved in both cases. The fact that the VMH appears to hold crucially for subject parasitic gaps adds further evidence of a more subtle nature for this conclusion. For further evidence, see Montalbetti 1984.

I have been assuming, following Taraldsen's original study of parasitic gaps, that there is a crucial distinction between the real gap, in the position more accessible to extraction, and the parasitic gap—that these are not simply "multiple gap" constructions. Evidence for this assumption is provided by Kearney (1983), who notes the following cases:

(140)
a. which books about himself did John file t [before Mary read e]
b. *which books about herself did John file t [before Mary read e]

Example (140a) is a normal parasitic gap construction, but (140b) is ungrammatical. It follows, then, that the *wh*-phrase in (141a), (141b) is extracted from the position of *t*, the real gap, not from the position of the parasitic gap *e*. As Taraldsen had originally assumed, the latter is truly "parasitic."

Further evidence that may bear on the presence of an operator in parasitic gap constructions is provided by Contreras (1984) and Hudson (1984). Previous literature had assumed that in a parasitic gap construction (141), the real gap *t* does not c-command the parasitic gap *e:*

(141)
O [NP [$_{VP}$ ...t...] [$_{Adjunct}$ ...e...]]

But it might be argued on the basis of binding-theoretic considerations that in fact *t* does c-command *e,* as illustrated by examples such as (142a–c):

(142)
a. they visited us [before we admitted those students]
b. we interviewed them [before we admitted those students]
c. we interviewed [their parents] [before we admitted those students]

In (142a) *they* cannot bind *those students,* which it c-commands, a typical instance of binding theory condition C. In (142c), however, this constraint does not hold because *their* does not c-command *those students.* In (142b) binding of *those students* by *them* appears to have a status intermediate between that of the ungrammatical (142a) and the grammatical (142c). If this fact is taken to show that in (142b) *them* does c-command *those students,* then *t* c-commands *e* in (141). The structure of (141), then, is either (143a) or (143b):

(143)
a. O [NP [$_{VP}$ ...t... [$_{Adjunct}$ ...e...]]]
b. O [NP [$_{VP}$[$_{VP'}$ ...t...] [$_{Adjunct}$ ...e...]]]

If the structure is (143a), then the Adjunct phrase is a sister to *t* and is c-commanded by *t.* If the structure is (143b), then the Adjunct phrase is within VP but outside of some "small VP" VP' and is perhaps "weakly c-commanded" by *t,* yielding a "weaker" violation of condition C of the binding theory in (142b). The latter possibility requires some sharpening of the notion of c-command of a sort that has been proposed in other connections.

In either case the anti-c-command requirement of earlier work would not be strictly correct, and again the analysis in Chomsky 1982, which takes the parasitic gap to be locally bound by the real operator O of (141), would be undermined. The problem is overcome if we assume the empty operator analysis. The question we now face, again, is one of determining the conditions on chain composition as in (130).

Engdahl (1984) and Hudson (1984) provide additional examples that appear to be incompatible with the anti-c-command requirement. Consider the sentence (144):

(144)
which men did the police warn t [$_{CP}$ that they were about to arrest e]

This has a parasitic gap interpretation, with *e* the parasitic gap licensed by the real gap *t.*[45] Here CP is a governed complement of *warn* and hence, it might be assumed, a sister to *warn,* so that *t* c-commands *e.* Then (144) would be another case violating the anti-c-command requirement, again leading to the conclusion that operator movement is involved in the parasitic gap construction.

Luigi Rizzi (personal communication) observes that the examples in (142), (144) are not entirely persuasive as counterevidence to the anti-c-command requirement. In both cases the phrase with the parasitic gap might be outside the immediate c-command domain of the real gap (as in (143b), and with a comparable analysis of (144) in accordance with Stowell's (1981) assumptions on Case resistance). Furthermore, the status of (142b) might be attributed to the often degraded character of backward pronominalization. We have no clear evidence, then, that the anti-c-command requirement on parasitic gaps of Chomsky 1982 and other studies must be rejected, though we have good evidence that two operator-headed chains are composed in parasitic gap constructions.

Consider the following examples with a structure similar to (144):

(145)
a. who did you tell t [that you would visit e]
b. who did you ask t [why you should visit e]
c. who did you ask t [how you should address e]
d. who did you convince t [that Tom should visit e]
e. who did you convince t [that Tom should visit Bill [before we talk to e]]
f. who did you convince t [that Tom should visit e [before we talk to e']]

Example (145a) is presumably on a par with (144). Examples (145b) and (145c) seem considerably worse under the intended interpretation. If so, the reason could be that the pre-IP position is filled by the *wh*-phrase in (145b), (145c), so that operator movement is barred. Case (145d) is more acceptable than (145e), suggesting that the operator in the *before*-phrase is too far from the real gap *t* for the chain composition procedure to operate. Example (145f), if acceptable, suggests that a double process of chain composition may have taken place. Further questions arise when we replace the clausal complement of *convince* with an infinitival phrase (for example, *who did you convince to visit Bill before we talked to*) or when we consider constructions such as (146a–c):

(146)
a. who did you believe [t to have visited Bill [before we talked to e]]
b. who did you believe [t visited Bill [before we talked to e]]
c. who did you warn t [e would visit Bill]

I will put aside these and many other similar questions that appear difficult to resolve, in part because the facts are often quite obscure.

Though many questions remain, I will assume that operator movement is involved in parasitic gap constructions, as discussed above, so that a parasitic gap, although truly parasitic on the real gap in Taraldsen's sense, is a "real gap" in its own chain, headed by an empty operator. The major question, then, is to determine the conditions under which chain composition can take place at S-Structure, in accordance with (130), repeated here:

(130)
If $\mathscr{C} = (\alpha_1,...,\alpha_n)$ is the chain of the real gap, and $\mathscr{C}' = (\beta_1,...,\beta_m)$ is the chain of the parasitic gap, then the "composed chain"

$(\mathscr{C},\mathscr{C}') = (\alpha_1,...,\alpha_n,\beta_1,...,\beta_m)$

is the chain associated with the parasitic gap construction and yields its interpretation.

A large class of cases would be handled by adapting the assumption of earlier work that chain composition is possible only if the anti-c-command requirement is satisfied: that is, the real gap may not c-command the parasitic gap. We cannot derive this condition exactly in the manner of Chomsky 1982, though similar arguments are possible. Thus, consider the requirement, mentioned above, that a variable must be free in the domain of the head of its chain, a formulation of condition C of the binding theory that suffices to block "improper movement" (see note 20). If this condition holds of composed chains, then the anti-c-command requirement follows. Or suppose that A-chains (chains headed by an A-position) must satisfy the following Chain Condition:[46]

(147)
A maximal A-chain $(\alpha_1,...,\alpha_n)$ has exactly one Case-marked position (namely, α_1) and exactly one θ-marked position (namely, α_n).

Assume now that the condition (147) holds of any chain $(\alpha_1,...,\alpha_n)$ where the links meet the c-command condition, hence uniformly for noncompound chains and for a subchain of a composed chain satisfying the c-command requirement for links. It then follows that the real gap cannot c-command the parasitic gap; otherwise, the result will be a maximal A-chain headed by the real gap and violating the Chain Condition (147).

Either of these approaches assumes that examples such as those in (142) and (144) do not violate the anti-c-command requirement. Let us consider alternatives that might be pursued if such examples do violate the anti-c-command requirement. One possibility is that for chain composition between $\mathscr{C}$ and $\mathscr{C}'$ to take place in (130), β_1 must be subjacent to α_n; then Subjacency will hold for each link of the composed chain $(\mathscr{C}, \mathscr{C}')$. This condition will distinguish between such cases as (148a) and (148b):

(148)
a. what did you file t [$_{PP}$ before [O [you read e]]]
b. *who [t [$_{VP}$ spoke to you [$_{PP}$ before [O [you met e]]]]]

In (148a) $\mathscr{C} = (what, t)$ and $\mathscr{C}' = (O, e)$ (omitting intermediate traces), and O is subjacent to t, separated from it by only one barrier—namely, PP. In (148b), however, two barriers separate O from t—namely, PP and VP. Here we cannot appeal to the successive cyclic option that in effect voids VP as a barrier in overt movement cases, since chain composition involves no movement.

The same principle will apply in more complex cases such as (123b), repeated here:

(123)
b. which papers did John decide [$_{PP}$ before O [reading e]] to tell his secretary [t' [t were unavailable]]

Again omitting several intermediate traces, (123b) has the two chains $\mathscr{C} = (which\ papers, t', t)$ and $\mathscr{C}' = (O, e)$, and O is subjacent to t; there is only one barrier—namely, PP—which includes O but not t.[47] In fact, of the adjunct cases discussed so far, only those of the form (144) with the subject taken as the real gap violate the condition that chain composition is admissible if the operator of $\mathscr{C}'$ is subjacent to the final term of $\mathscr{C}$:

(149)
*who t [$_{VP}$ warned the men [$_{CP}$ that they were about to arrest e]]

Here only VP is a barrier for the operator of $\mathscr{C}'$, so that the subjacency condition on chain composition is satisfied though the sentence is ungrammatical.

Though this approach comes rather close to what is required, still it seems incorrect, not only because of the residual empirical problems but also because the failure of c-commanding subjects to license parasitic gaps, as in (148b), is a far stronger effect than subjacency. In fact, it has the extreme character of a government violation of the ECP variety. Suppose, then, that we slightly modify the approach just sketched, introducing the notion "0-subjacency" defined earlier (see (59)): in chain composition as in (130), forming ($\mathscr{C}$, $\mathscr{C}'$), the head of $\mathscr{C}'$ must be 0-subjacent to the final element of $\mathscr{C}$. Thus, β_1 must be 0-subjacent to α_n in (130).

The property of 0-subjacency is essentially government minus the c-command requirement, and we might suppose that this fact explains the rigid character of violations. The intuitive sense of the proposed condition is that in a composed chain ($\mathscr{C}$, $\mathscr{C}'$), not only must each link of $\mathscr{C}$ and $\mathscr{C}'$ satisfy the weak 1-subjacency condition as in any chain, but the two chains must be linked under an even stronger 0-subjacency condition akin in its properties to government.

This revision accommodates (149) straightforwardly, since a barrier separates the operator of the parasitic gap from the real gap. But a problem arises with respect to the standard example (148a):

(148)
a. what did you file t [$_{PP}$ before [O [you read e]]]

Here O is separated from t by the barrier PP and is therefore not 0-subjacent to it. Notice, however, that nothing prevents O from adjoining to PP, yielding (150):

(150)
what did you file t [$_{PP}$ O [$_{PP}$ before [e' [you read e]]]]

Here O is indeed 0-subjacent to t, as required.

In discussing the adjunct island case of the CED, we ignored this option, but illegitimately on our assumptions, since it was available. This has the effect of voiding the Adjunct Condition entirely. Thus, consider again the examples (63a–b):

(63)
a. he is the person to whom [$_{IP}$ they left [before speaking t]]
b. he is the person who [$_{IP}$ they left [before speaking to t]] (before meeting t)

In (63a) *to whom* can adjoin to the adjunct *before*-phrase, then moving to its final position, crossing no barriers at any point; the same is true of (63b). In fact, as we saw, (63b) is fairly acceptable, whereas (63a) is unacceptable. We assumed that the relative acceptability of (63b) was the problem, taking it to be a Subjacency violation. Suppose, however, that the analysis just suggested is correct. Then it is not the acceptability of (63b) but rather the unacceptability of (63a) that is the problem. Perhaps only NP is permitted to adjoin to the PP adjunct *before*-phrase. If some plausible reason can be found for this, then we might assume the option of attachment to PP in successive cyclic movement to be available, as would be expected on our earlier assumptions.

We must, however, ensure that an ECP violation still results when an adjunct is extracted from an adjunct phrase, as in (65):

(65)
a. *how did you leave [before fixing the car t]
b. *who left [before fixing the car how]
c. who left [before fixing what]

This will follow even allowing adjunction to PP under either of two assumptions: (1) only NP is permitted to adjoin to the PP adjunct position (see above); or (2) we define "government" in terms of domination, as in (14), rather than in terms of exclusion, as in (18). The latter assumption raises numerous problems, as we have seen.

This account still leaves questions open concerning subject parasitic constructions such as (132), (134a). If the 0-subjacency condition on chain composition is correct and if subject parasitic gap constructions fall under it, then the empty operator must move out of the subject position (which is a barrier) at S-Structure, where chain composition is licensed. As noted earlier, several possibilities might be pursued, but the question remains obscure.

Many further questions arise in addition to those already noted. For example, it is clear, as Luigi Rizzi (personal communication) has pointed out, that the subject of a small clause cannot license a parasitic gap, as illustrated in (151):

(151)

a. I consider [John [$_{AP}$ absolutely certain [$_{CP}$ that we can help him]]]

b. *who do you consider [t [$_{AP}$ absolutely certain [$_{CP}$ that we can help e]]]

The result follows at once from the anti-c-command requirement but will follow from the 0-subjacency condition on chain formation only if we assume that the empty operator of the parasitic gap does not move beyond CP; this would follow from the basic condition (6) on adjunction if AP is taken to be the argument selected by *consider* and heading the small clause, as in Stowell's theory, assumed earlier.

Rizzi also notes the following pair in Italian:

(152)

a. che studente hai convinto t [che puoi aiutare e]

a'. which student did you convince t [that you could help e]

b. *che studente [α è stato convinto t [che puoi aiutare e]]

b'. which student [α was convinced t [that you would help e]]

Example (152a) is an acceptable parasitic gap construction on a par with (144), but (152b) is ungrammatical. Here α is the empty category subject permitted in this null subject language. The anti-c-command requirement could be construed so as to permit (152a) while excluding (152b) if we make the standard assumption that α is coindexed with t, forming a kind of chain, and assume the structure (153) for the VP so that t does not c-command CP:

(153)

[$_{VP}$[convinto t] [$_{CP}$ che puoi aiutare e]]

To accommodate these facts within the 0-subjacency hypothesis would require a modification of the chain composition condition to (154):

(154)

The operator of the parasitic gap must be 0-subjacent to the head of the A-chain of the real gap.

Clearly many questions remain open and are well worth pursuing, since the parasitic gap constructions are particularly revealing with respect to UG for reasons discussed in Chomsky 1982.

Summarizing the discussion of parasitic gaps, we have strong evidence that they involve chain composition with an operator binding the parasitic gap. Chain composition is subject to a further condition, perhaps the requirement that a variable be free in the domain of the head of its chain or the general Chain Condition (147) as construed earlier, yielding the anti-c-command condition in either case, or perhaps a requirement that the operator binding the parasitic gap be "sufficiently close" to the real gap, perhaps under the condition of 0-subjacency. A number of properties of the construction, some fairly intricate, then follow.

11. A-Chains

So far I have restricted attention to $\overline{\text{A}}$-movement of maximal projections, apart from brief mention of V-raising to C, as in (155):

(155)
[how tall] is John

Let us now turn to the question of head movement, asking how it might fit into the proposed framework. The optimal assumption would be that movement of zero-level categories falls under the principles that apply to movement of maximal projections: in particular, the trace must be properly governed. Let us examine the consequence of this assumption, within the framework already sketched.

It is clear that head movement is highly "local" and that violations of locality are far stronger than Subjacency violations. Thus, consider the D-Structure representation underlying (155):

(156)
$[_{CP} \dots [_{C'} C [_{IP} NP [_{I'} I [_{VP} V \dots]]]]]$

First V (= *be*) moves to the head position I of IP, amalgamating with I, and then this newly formed inflected element V_I moves to C, the head position of CP, yielding (155) after *wh*-movement. Since I is lexically identified as an affix in (156), movement of V to I forming V_I is permissible—indeed, it is obligatory, since otherwise the affix would lack a bearer. Thus, V cannot move directly to the position of C in (156). If I were a nonaffix—for example, the modal *will*—then V could not adjoin to I, but movement to the position of C must still be barred, or we could derive (157):

(157)
[how tall]$_j$ be$_i$ $[_{IP}$ John $[_{IP}$ will $[_{VP} t_i\ t_j]]]$

In general, the V head of VP can reach the head position C of CP only if it first passes through the head position I of IP, amalgamating with inflection.

Since movement of V is possible, its trace must be properly governed, and since the movement is local, this proper government must be by antecedent government, not θ-government. It follows that V-raising as in (155) is permissible, but V-lowering is not, and that such head raising must be sufficiently local as to guarantee antecedent government.

Notice that V is not θ-marked by I; if it were, V would be properly governed and "long movement" would be permitted. This conclusion is inconsistent with the combination of two previous assumptions: (i) that I θ-marks its VP complement; (ii) that qualification (35) holds on the Sisterhood Condition for θ-government. One or the other of these must therefore be abandoned. We will see directly that there is good reason to preserve (i) and that (ii) is untenable. We therefore maintain (i) and abandon (ii), thus concluding that V is not θ-marked by I, as required.

Given these assumptions, V-raising to yield (157) produces an ECP violation, since VP and (by inheritance) IP are barriers. If VP were L-marked by *will,* VP would not be a barrier, nor would IP, since it can be a barrier only by inheritance, and direct raising of *be* to yield (157) would be legitimate. We therefore must maintain the assumption that I does not L-mark its complement; L-marking is restricted to lexical categories. Note that the illicit movement in (157) cannot be blocked by the Minimality Condition, because of the defective character of I'.

Suppose that first V moves to the head position I of IP, amalgamating with I to form V_I, and then V_I moves to C. The movement of V_I to C crosses no barriers to government, since IP can be a barrier only by inheritance. Consider movement from V to I, yielding (158):

(158)
$[_{I'} V_I [_{VP} t ...]]$

Movement from V to I crosses VP, which should be a barrier to antecedent government of *t* by V_I. But the fact that this movement is legitimate shows that V_I must L-mark VP in (158), voiding barrierhood.

The concepts relevant here are L-marking and θ-government, which we had construed as follows (ignoring the qualification (35)):

(47)

Where α is a lexical category, α L-marks β iff β agrees with the head of γ that is θ-governed by α.

(27)

α θ-governs β iff α is a zero-level category that θ-marks β, and α, β are sisters.

Thus, a lexical category α L-marks a category β that it θ-governs as well as the head of β, and also the specifier of β if β is IP or CP.

Prior to V-raising, I does not L-mark VP in (158) because it is not lexical. After V-raising, the newly formed element V_I is lexical and therefore L-marks VP. This conclusion crucially rests on the assumption that I θ-marks VP; thus, I fails to L-mark VP, voiding barrierhood, solely because I is not lexical. We therefore conclude, as before, that I does θ-mark its VP complement and that L-marking is restricted to lexical categories.

Since V_I L-marks VP in (158), raising of V to the position of the θ-governor I of VP is legitimate, producing no ECP violation; VP is no longer a barrier for the trace of V, which is therefore properly governed by the raised V.

More generally, consider the options for movement of a lexical category β, the head of γ, where α is a zero-level category:

(159)

$...\alpha...[_\gamma ...\beta...]...$

As we have seen, β can only raise to the position of a zero-level category in which it will antecedent-govern its trace. Suppose that α governs γ. Then β cannot raise "beyond" α by virtue of the Minimality Condition, except in the case of $\alpha = I$ with γ its VP complement (given the defective character of I'). But here too, as we have just seen in the case of (157), such movement is barred for β, the V head of γ. Hence, β cannot raise beyond α when α governs γ.

The question of head movement, then, reduces to the question of when β in (159) can move to the position of α, which governs γ. Suppose α θ-governs γ or L-marks γ. Then the amalgamated element β-α formed by raising β to α will L-mark γ, so that γ is not a barrier for the trace of β and raising is possible. Suppose that α neither θ-governs nor L-marks γ. Then γ will be a barrier and raising will be impossible unless γ is L-marked in some other manner, so that it has a governor apart from α but one that does not invoke the Minimality Condition, a condition that can arise only under SPEC-head agreement in IP or CP (see examples (44), (48), (49)). Putting this contingency aside, we conclude that β in (159) can only move to the position of α, where α either θ-governs or L-marks γ. Thus, if β = V and α = I, β can raise to α, as in the cases discussed earlier. And if α = V and γ is its NP or PP complement, then β (= N or P) can raise to the position of α, as in noun and preposition incorporation structures, but the head of an adjunct or non-L-marked subject cannot raise to α.[48] Notice also that if β = I and α = C in (159), then I, though nonlexical, can raise to the position C, since IP is not a barrier. These conclusions can be expressed as the general Head Movement Constraint (160):[49]

(160)
Movement of a zero-level category β is restricted to the position of a head α that governs the maximal projection γ of β, where α θ-governs or L-marks γ if $\alpha \neq$ C.

Recall that these conclusions follow on the assumption that β, the head of γ, is not θ-governed in (159); that is, the qualification (35) to the Sisterhood Condition on θ-government cannot be sustained. The specific discussion so far has been restricted to α = I and γ = VP in (159), where I is assumed to θ-govern VP; the desired conclusions for V-raising follow if the qualification (35) is abandoned. But we need not restrict ourselves to this case, with its questionable assumption that I θ-marks VP. Suppose that γ in (159) is NP and that α is a verb θ-governing γ. Since the constraint (160) holds for noun incorporation (that is, the head β of γ can raise to the position of α but not beyond), it follows that β cannot be θ-governed by α. Hence, we must abandon the qualification (35) if θ-government suffices for proper government.

We noted earlier that the two assumptions (i) (that I θ-marks its VP complement) and (ii) (that qualification (35) holds) could not be jointly sustained. We now have found reasons to maintain (i) and independent reasons to reject (35). We conclude, then, that (i) holds and that the strict Sisterhood Condition for θ-government is maintained; that is, θ-marking does not "percolate" from a category to its head.

This conclusion is inconsistent with Stowell's (1981) theory of empty complementizer distribution. It therefore seems that we must abandon this analysis, at least in the terms formulated earlier. See also note 28.

We have assumed that V-raising of V to I in (158) yields a chain (161), where V_I and t are coindexed:

(161)
(V_I, t)

A convention is required to ensure that (161) is actually a chain, with coindexing. Let us adopt the fairly standard assumption that the relevant properties of the raised V, including index, "percolate" to V_I. Then (161) qualifies as a properly formed chain.

Suppose that V raises to the position of I and perhaps subsequently to C in (156), forming a chain $\mathscr{C} = (V_I, \ldots, t)$ headed by the amalgamated inflected verb V_I and terminating in the D-Structure position t of V. Then the head V_I of $\mathscr{C}$ governs the subject NP. But we do not want to permit the verbal element of V_I to either θ-mark or Case-mark the subject. Regarding a chain as an abstract representation of its head, we may assume, for present purposes, that only the terminal D-Structure position in the chain retains the capacity to θ-mark or Case-mark.[50] Other approaches are possible; the relevant issues involve a range of constructions and typologically different languages (causatives, VSO languages, etc.) that raise questions beyond the bounds of this discussion.

Consider, then, a structure such as (162):

(162)
who are$_i$ [$_{IP}$[$_{NP}$ pictures of e] t$'_i$ [$_{VP}$ t$_i$ on sale]]

Here $\mathscr{C} = (are, t', t)$ is the chain of *are*, with t' in the I position and t in the D-Structure position of head of VP; e is the trace of *who*. Since the NP subject is not L-marked by t, the sole element of $\mathscr{C}$ that retains the capacity to L-mark, we obtain the CED effect, as required.

In examples (155) and (162) the verbal head itself raised to I, forming V_I, then raised further to the head C of the clause CP. If an element of I raises to C—say, a modal as in (163)—then the VP retains its status as a barrier under our current assumptions:

(163)
what$_i$ will$_j$ [$_{IP}$ John t$_j$ [$_{VP}$ read t$_i$]]

To complete the discussion, it is necessary to provide a specific analysis of the auxiliary system, including *do*-support and aspectual elements as in (164):

(164)
John has been reading a book

For concreteness, let us assume that *do* is inserted to bear the features of AGR under the familiar conditions and that the aspectual elements are "defective" verbs that select but do not θ-mark VP.[51] Hence, aspectual elements do not L-mark their complements, though when an aspectual element raises to I, forming V_I, the latter does L-mark its complement. We resort to VP-adjunction to void barrierhood of the internal VPs.

It follows now that (165) can be derived from (156), after which V_I can be moved to the head C of CP:

(156)
$[_{CP} \ldots [_{C'} \text{ C } [_{IP} \text{ NP } [_{I'} \text{ I } [_{VP} \text{ V } \ldots]]]]]$

(165)
$[_{CP} \ldots [_{C'} \text{ C } [_{IP} \text{ NP } [_{I'} V_I [_{VP} \text{ t } \ldots]]]]]$

The Head Movement Constraint (160) prevents raising to I of any element other than the initial verb of the VP governed by I.

This analysis requires that we prevent adjunction of a lexical category to a maximal projection, as in (166):

(166)
$[_{VP} \text{ V } [_{VP} \text{ t } \ldots]]$

If this were possible, then V could raise to the head of CP without passing through I, violating no conditions. It seems, then, that adjunction to maximal projections is an option restricted to maximal projections, just as substitution for a maximal projection is. This conclusion, a kind of generalization of Emonds's Structure-Preserving Hypothesis, would follow if we were to regard movement of a lexical category as analogous to NP-movement, barring (166) either on the grounds that *t* is an unlicensed free variable or that there is "improper movement," with *t* ultimately bound in the domain of the head of its chain. Thus, head-to-head movement creates an A-chain, whereas movement of a head to an adjoined position would create an $\overline{A}$-chain. On these (rather reasonable) assumptions, the main properties of head movement follow.

Suppose that the VP complement of V_I in (158) includes a parasitic gap construction, as in the standard example (167a) with the S-Structure representation (167b), where *e* is the real gap and *e'* the parasitic gap:

(167)

a. the book that John filed without reading

b. the book that $[_{IP}$ John $[_{I'}$ filed$_i$ $[_{VP}$ t$_i$ e]] [without O [reading e']]]

Recall that we considered two approaches to chain composition for such constructions, one based on the anti-c-command requirement, another based on 0-subjacency. Under the latter approach, VP in (167) must remain a barrier for chain composition even though raising of V to I has removed its barrierhood. One can imagine ways to overcome the apparent inconsistency, but it provides an additional (highly theory-internal) reason to suppose that the anti-c-command requirement is indeed the correct one.

It remains to consider the properties of NP-movement, as in raising and passive:

(168)

a.   John seems [t to be intelligent]

b.   John was killed t

c.   *John seems that it appears [t to be intelligent]

d.   *John seems that it is considered [t to be intelligent]

As we have seen, (168c) and (168d) (= (41)) are excluded as ECP violations, but why are (168a) and (168b) permitted?

Consider more closely the structure of (168a), after V-raising:

(169)

John$_i$ $[_\alpha$ seem-I] $[_{VP}$ t$_j$ $[_{IP}$ t$_i$ to be intelligent]]

Here α is the antecedent of t_j, with index j. VP is a barrier for t_i by the Minimality Condition. Thus, movement of *John* to the subject position is barred. The corresponding case of *wh*-movement is not barred in this way;[52] in this case adjunction to VP is possible, voiding the barrier to proper government since the adjoined element is not excluded by VP. But the option of VP-adjunction is not available for raising of the NP *John* to matrix subject position; this would be a case of "improper movement," barred, we have assumed, by the requirement that the $\overline{A}$-bound trace must be A-free in the domain of the head of its chain, a subcase of condition C of the binding theory. The same considerations incorrectly bar (168b).

A solution to this problem is suggested by the association of the subject of IP with its head I, which we took to be a case of "feature sharing" entering into L-marking (see (47)), one case being the sharing of an abstract feature F, between specifier and I. So far, we have been distinguishing chain coindexing from the feature sharing of agreement. Suppose that we now assimilate these relations, assuming that the abstract feature F is an index shared in SPEC-head agreement and that it is the same index that appears in a chain; in other words, indexing is unique.[53] It now follows that $i = j$ in (169), since the NP subject is chain-coindexed with its trace and also agrees with *seem-I*.

In (169), then, t_i is governed by and coindexed with t_j, the trace of the raised V. Under a slight extension of the notion of antecedent government, it would follow that t_i is antecedent-governed by t_j, thus properly governed by it. Suppose that we now extend chain coindexing to include this case, in effect treating t_i as the final element of an extended chain—in other words, allowing the chain itself, via its terminal element, to properly govern t_i by antecedent government. We thus define "chain coindexing" as follows:

(170)
a. $\mathscr{C} = (\alpha_1,...,\alpha_n,\beta)$ is an extended chain if $(\alpha_1,...,\alpha_n)$ is a chain with index i and β has index i.
b. Chain coindexing holds of the links of an extended chain.

Since chain coindexing under government suffices for proper government (see (31)), the final element of an extended chain $\mathscr{C}$ is properly governed if it is governed by the terminal element of the chain. In particular, independently of the status of VP as a barrier in (169), t_i is properly governed by t_j in the extended chain (α,t_j,t_i).

Consider the effect of this analysis on (168c), repeated here:

(168)
c. [$_{IP'}$ John seems that [$_{IP}$ it appears [t to be intelligent]]]

Here the index of the chain (*John,t*) is shared with *seem* after V-raising in IP'; however, the trace of *seem* does not govern t, so the latter yields an ECP violation. Note that we must assume that I of IP and I' of IP' are not "accidentally coindexed"; if they are, the trace of *appear* will properly govern t. Thus, a general convention, perhaps derivable from more general considerations, must be that coindexing of clausal heads cannot arise "accidentally" but must be contingent on some grammatical process such as successive cyclic NP-movement.

The same considerations will account for (168d), so that the only problematic case is now the simple passive, (168b), with the more articulated structure (171) after V-raising, where α has the index j and heads the chain (α, t_j):

(171)
John$_i$ [$_\alpha$ be-I] [$_{VP'}$ t$_j$ [$_{VP}$ killed t$_i$]]

The question is: how is t_i properly governed? This case is different from (168a), since in (171) t_i is θ-governed (hence, properly governed) by *kill*. This could be the right answer, but only if other principles ensure that "super-raising" is impossible in such structures as (172):

(172)
*a man seems [there to be killed t]

On the other hand, if (172) is an ECP violation on a par with (168c–d), then proper government of t_i by its θ-governor must be blocked in (171). Let us explore this possibility, assuming that θ-government does not suffice for proper government of an A-bound trace.

Returning to (171), we observe that as in (168a), α has the index i because of SPEC-head agreement with the matrix subject *John*, so that $j = i$. Consider now the VP' substructure of (171):

(173)
[$_{VP'}$ t$_j$ [$_{VP}$ killed t$_i$]]

This could be regarded as a special case of the "adjunction structure" (174):

(174)
[$_\beta$ α [$_\beta$ ...]]

If so, then t_j governs t_i in (171), since it is not excluded by the verb phrase with the segments (VP', VP). Since t_j is also coindexed with t_i ($i = j$), the latter is properly governed in the extended chain (be, t_j, t_i), as required, independently of θ-government by *killed*.

Note that we are assuming that in (171) VP is a segment of the verb phrase, not a category in itself that excludes t_j; otherwise, the Minimality Condition will block government of t_i by t_j. Thus, the structure (174) counts as an "adjunction structure" whether it is base-generated or formed by an adjunction rule, and again we assume that V' need not appear in VP (see (3)).[54]

A further question arises in the case of NP-movement from the position of NP in (175), where I is a modal or infinitival head lacking AGR, as in (176):

(175)

...I [$_{VP}$ V* NP...]

(176)

a. John will be killed t

b. John seems [t' to be believed [t to have left]]

In (176a) *be* does not raise to I, forming *will-be* (or *be-will*); if it did, subsequent raising to C would yield (177):

(177)

*will-be (be-will) John killed

But if the preceding analysis is to be extended to (176a), it must be that *be* is nevertheless coindexed with *t* as a reflex of the movement of *John* to subject position; then chain coindexing will hold between the trivial chain (*be*) and *t,* under (170). The assumption we need is that independent of raising, there is head-head agreement (index sharing) between I and the aspectual verbs of V* in (175); hence, there is (indirect) agreement between the subject and each aspectual verb of VP, as a reflex of SPEC-head agreement. This assumption will suffice to permit NP-movement in (176a).

Note that if the relation of head-head agreement extends to all verbs in V* of (175), including the main verb, then we need not appeal to the adjunction argument just sketched for (171), (173), since t_i will be antecedent-governed by the trivial chain (*killed*).

In the case of (176b) there is no comparable direct evidence that *be* does not raise to I (= *to*). If it does not, then the argument just sketched for modals will suffice to permit successive cyclic movement; if it does, then the analysis for verbs that raise to I applies. Recall again that "accidental coindexing," not resulting from some specific grammatical process, is barred by convention, so that there can be no "super-raising" avoiding successive cyclic movement.

If this line of argument is correct, we need no recourse to θ-government to permit passive, and if indeed θ-government does not yield proper government for A-bound trace, then "super-raising" as in (172) yields an ECP violation on a par with (168c).

Suppose, then, that for A-bound trace, proper government reduces to antecedent government, θ-government being excluded. Recall that given the option of VP-adjunction that we have assumed throughout, the object of a verb is always antecedent-governed after A̅-movement, namely, by the trace adjoined to the VP of which it is the object.

Therefore, θ-government can also be eliminated from the definition of "proper government" for $\bar{A}$-bound trace governed by a verb. For verb-complement structures, then, proper government can be reduced to antecedent government by chain coindexing.

Consider what this approach entails with regard to raising to subject of adjectives, as in (178):

(178)
a.   John is [$_{AP}$ likely [$_\alpha$ t to win]]
b.   *John is [$_{AP}$ probable [$_\alpha$ t to win]]

Given that the examples of (179) are ungrammatical, it is reasonable to conclude that α in (178), (179) is IP, not CP, hence not a barrier to government of PRO:

(179)
a.   *it is likely [$_\alpha$ PRO to win]
b.   *it is probable [$_\alpha$ PRO to win]

The similarity in meaning of *likely* and *probable* suggests that a rather marginal lexical property may be what distinguishes these constructions (other examples appear to support this conclusion). Hence, presumably one of them is a marked structure, to be accounted for by some idiosyncratic mechanism, whereas the other should be accounted for on principled grounds. Which is the marked case?

Assume that the copula, like aspectual elements, does not θ-mark its complement AP, so that AP is not L-marked and therefore is a barrier for t in (178). If so, it is (178a) that is the marked case. SPEC-head agreement holds between *John* and the raised verb *be-I,* but *likely* and *probable* share no features with the subject, I, or t. Therefore, the examples of (178) should be ECP violations. It is (179a) that requires some special stipulation, perhaps marked coindexing of *be* and *likely* (a kind of restructuring), so that chain coindexing (hence, proper government) holds of the extended chain (*likely,t*). The situation in languages similar to English, which appear to lack constructions such as (178a), supports this conclusion concerning markedness. We might assume, then, that a lexical property of some generality accounts for CP-reduction (selection of IP rather than CP by the adjective at LF), yielding the unmarked paradigm illustrated by (178b) and (179).

The assumption that the copula does not θ-mark its complement[55] is required on this analysis to permit adjunct extraction in (180a), yielding (180b):

(180)
a. the meat is [$_{AP}$ cooked [how well]]
b. [how well] is the meat cooked t

Proper government of the trace requires adjunction to AP (otherwise, it will be blocked by the Minimality Condition); and our general assumption (see (6)) has been that adjunction is possible only to nonarguments.

To summarize, we have been led to the following conclusions, on the assumption that the trace of a zero-level category must be properly governed:

1. VP is θ-marked by I.
2. Only lexical categories are L-markers, so that VP is not L-marked by I.
3. θ-government is restricted to sisterhood without the qualification (35).
4. Only the terminus of an X^0-chain can θ-mark or Case-mark.
5. Head-to-head movement forms an A-chain.
6. SPEC-head agreement and chains involve the same indexing.
7. Chain coindexing holds of the links of an extended chain.
8. There is no accidental coindexing of I.
9. I-V coindexing is a form of head-head agreement; if it is restricted to aspectual verbs, then base-generated structures of the form (174) count as adjunction structures.
10. Possibly, a verb does not properly govern its θ-marked complement.

The consequences of these assumptions are ramified and there are many special cases to check to determine whether they are acceptable. If something of this sort proves correct, then we can eliminate θ-government from the definition of "proper government" at least for the case of verb-complement structures. In the case of $\overline{A}$-movement (e.g., *wh*-movement), adjunction to VP will always yield proper government by chain coindexing, and in the case of A-movement (raising and passive) the trace will be antecedent-governed independently of θ-marking. It would also follow that the object of *kill* in (176a) may not undergo "long movement" merely because it is θ-marked by *kill*. It may be that other considerations conspire to bar this in any event, but we would now have a direct ECP argument. For a large range of central cases of the ECP, then, the principle can be reduced to antecedent government and treated simply as a "chain phenomenon," which would explain at once why it does not hold for the empty categories pro and PRO.

The idea that the ECP is in effect a chain phenomenon underlies the approach to the principle developed by Richard Kayne and others under somewhat different assumptions. To pursue it further in the framework assumed here, it would be necessary to consider the consequences for complements of P, A, and N, where no raising or coindexing of head takes place (there is no counterpart to the I-V relation). Many questions arise: with regard to preposition stranding, AP-adjunction, "internal" antecedent government of complement of NP (perhaps by a property of the specifier; see Torrego 1985 and references cited), and so forth.

---

12. Some Further Problems

Huang (1982) presents the following paradigm, which should, it would seem, be accounted for by a proper formulation of the concepts of subjacency and proper government:

(181)
a. which city did you witness [$_{NP}$ the [destruction of t]]
b. of which city did you witness [$_{NP}$ the [destruction t]]
c. *which city did you meet [$_{NP}$ the man [$_{PP}$ from t]]
d. *from which city did you meet [$_{NP}$ the man t]

LF-movement is possible in a structure corresponding to (181c)—compare (182)—indicating on Huang's assumptions that the problem here involves not the ECP but the CED (Subjacency):

(182)
who met [$_{NP}$ the man [$_{PP}$ from which city]]

Huang argues that in (182) *which city* is properly governed by *from* and is attracted at LF by *who*, Subjacency being irrelevant at this level.

Cases (181a) and (181b) are as expected, assuming proper government internal to NP, since there are no barriers. In (181c) PP is not θ-governed and is therefore a barrier. Since NP inherits barrierhood, two barriers are crossed and a Subjacency violation results (assuming, now, no adjunction to PP). This explanation does not carry over to (181d), which would therefore have to be regarded as an ECP violation, suggesting that it should be a "stronger" violation than (181c). Perhaps the Minimality Condition might be extended so that *the man* will count as a "closer governor" and NP will be a barrier.

Some other structures that seem similar to (181) behave differently:

(183)

a. this is the city that I met [$_{NP}$ three people [$_{PP}$ from t]]
b. which city did you meet [$_{NP}$ more people [$_{PP}$ from t]] (London or Paris)

The contrast between (181c–d) and (183a–b) is reminiscent of the contrast between (184) and (185):

(184)

a. *who did you see that picture of
b. *who did you see John's picture of

(185)

a. who did you see three pictures of
b. who did you see more pictures of (John or Bill)

Relative judgments appear comparable in the two paradigms, suggesting that a "specificity condition" not considered here may be relevant throughout. In any event, this configuration remains in part unexplained, along with other properties of extraction from NP.

We have touched several times on the question whether "government" should be defined in terms of domination (inclusion) as in (14) or exclusion as in (18). The difference relates to adjunction structures such as (186):

(186)

[$_{\beta'}$ α [$_{\beta}$ ...γ...]]

If "government" is defined in terms of inclusion, then α does not govern γ since there is a barrier—namely, β—that includes γ but not α. If "government" is defined in terms of exclusion, then α does govern γ.

Suppose that an adjunct appears within VP, as in (187), assuming now the theory of predication proposed by Williams (1980). The well-formed D-Structure representation (187a) (compare *John ate the meat raw*) yields the S-Structure representation (187b):

(187)

a. John I [$_{VP}$ eat the meat [how raw]]
b. *how raw did John [$_{VP}$ eat the meat t]

We might explain (187b) on the grounds that *wh*-movement crosses the barrier VP so that *t* is not properly governed, yielding an ECP violation.

Suppose, however, that we take the option of VP-adjunction in forming (187b), deriving the structure (188):

(188)
*how raw did John [$_{VP'}$ t' [$_{VP}$ eat the meat t]]

The verb phrase in (188) is an instance of (186); it includes *t* but not *t'* and thus remains a barrier for government as desired, if we define "government" in terms of inclusion. More generally, it follows from this definition that (189):

(189)
An adjunct can adjoin only to IP.

The reason is that only IP is not a barrier by virtue of being a BC (see (26b)). We have assumed that operators such as *wh*-phrases cannot adjoin to IP; therefore, if (189) is correct, it may be that it is an instance of something more general. But we now have problems elsewhere—for example, with regard to adjunct movement, which, as discussed earlier, requires the definition (18) in terms of exclusion (see (55)–(57)), along with other cases discussed above.

Compare (187) with (190):

(190)
a. how clean did John pick the bone t
b. how red did John paint the house t
c. how angry did John make his friends t

Here movement of the *wh*-phrase requires adjunction to VP and the definition of "government" in terms of exclusion, not inclusion, to yield proper government. These cases may differ from (187) in that in (190) there is a relation between the matrix verb and the *wh*-phrase; in (190c) under a small clause analysis with the fronted AP as the selected head, in (190a) because of the lexical character of *pick clean* (as distinct from *eat raw*), and in (190b) possibly for the same reason (note that picking-clean is something that can be done to a bone and painting-red is something that can be done to a house, but eating-raw is not something that can be done to meat).[56] The distinction between (187) and (190) therefore suggests that some kind of connection between α and a lexical category may be required, over and above antecedent government, for the trace of α to satisfy proper government, as suggested by Osvaldo Jaeggli, Luigi Rizzi, and Esther Torrego in current work.

Notice that subject-oriented predicates also do not undergo *wh*-movement, just as object-oriented ones such as *raw* in (187) do not. Consider (191b), derived from (191a):[57]

(191)
a.   John [left the room] [(how) angry]
b.   *how angry did John [leave the room] t

These contrast with adjunct movement as in (192):

(192)
a.   why did John [leave the room] t
b.   how did John [fix the car] t

The same is true of subject-oriented adverbs:

(193)
a.   John cleverly [read the book]
b.   John [read the book cleverly]
c.   how cleverly did John read the book

The interpretation of (193c) indicates that it derives from (193b), not (193a): thus, (193c) asks about the manner in which John read the book, not about how clever John was to read the book.

Presumably (191) and (193) fall together, as contrasted with (192). The relevant difference might again reduce to the requirement that proper government satisfy a relation to a lexical category over and above antecedent government; thus, in (193b) *cleverly* is lexically governed by *read,* but there is no such relation in cases (191), (193a). Examples of adjunct movement, as in (192), would then be exempt from this requirement for some reason or would involve a relation to an appropriate zero-level category, either the verb or I (possibly *how* and *why* might be distinguished in this connection, as has sometimes been proposed). Although we have no definite explanation for these facts, there is a plausible line of inquiry. We still have no good reason, then, to support the choice of the definition (14) in terms of inclusion, and a number of strong reasons to choose the alternative (18) in terms of exclusion.

A number of problems arise concerning the structure of gerunds. Consider (194a–b):

(194)

a. John regretted [$_\alpha$ PRO losing the race]

b. John believed [$_{IP}$[$_\alpha$ PRO losing the race] to be a tragedy]

In (194a) the category α is θ-marked by *regret* and is therefore not a BC, but PRO nevertheless is not governed if we assume government to be the crucial property determining distribution of PRO, as in Chomsky 1981, 1985, for example. Similarly, in (194b) we have assumed that α is L-marked and therefore not a BC or barrier for PRO so that IP is also not a barrier for PRO, though again PRO must be protected from government. It may be that gerunds have the structure of an NP dominating a clause so that the NP is a barrier by inheritance.

Another problem relates to the conclusion that there is empty operator movement in the parasitic gap constructions. This runs counter to an argument by Stowell (1981) that gerunds do not have a COMP position (in our present terms, that they are IP rather than CP). Thus, Stowell notes that *wh*-phrases cannot be attached to gerunds, as illustrated in (195):

(195)

a.   I remembered that he read the book

b.   I remembered his reading the book

c.   I remembered why he read the book

d.   *I remembered why his reading the book

The foregoing analysis suggests that gerunds do have a COMP position. The problem is now shifted from explaining why they are exceptionally IP rather than CP to explaining why overt *wh*-phrases cannot appear in the COMP position. A further and long-standing problem is to explain in a principled way why gerunds share properties of clauses and NPs.

Consider the small clause structure (196):

(196)

I consider [$_{AP'}$ Bill [$_{AP}$ angry at Tom]]

Here the matrix verb θ-marks its complement AP'. What is the status of the AP "head" of the small clause? If AP is L-marked, then it is not a barrier, so that (197) is not a Subjacency violation:

(197)

who do you consider [$_{AP'}$ Bill [$_{AP}$ angry at t]]

Since (197) is grammatical, we conclude that AP is L-marked in (196), as it will be by the definition (47), repeated here, assuming AP to be the head of AP':

(47)
Where α is a lexical category, α L-marks β iff β agrees with the head of γ that is θ-governed by α.

It is necessary to ensure that t is properly governed in (197). If the ECP is reduced to a chain property of antecedent government along the lines of the discussion in section 11, then adjunction to AP is necessary to ensure proper government; otherwise, the Minimality Condition will prevent antecedent government. If, as we have assumed throughout, adjunction is only possible to nonarguments (see (6)), then AP is not θ-marked in (196), (197), though it is the "head" of the θ-marked construction AP'. This again suggests (though it does not precisely require) that we drop the qualification (35) on θ-government. Note that it is now irrelevant whether AP is L-marked, since extraction will be possible successive-cyclically.

At the outset, I mentioned that within the general framework developed here one might regard government as blocked by one barrier or two maximal projections. Assuming the Minimality Condition, these assumptions yield different conclusions in two major cases: (i) Exceptional Case-marking constructions and (ii) constructions that involve adjunct movement over a single maximal projection that is a barrier. Let us consider these cases in turn.

Consider first Exceptional Case-marking constructions such as (198a–b):

(198)
a. John expects [[stories about Bill] to be interesting]
b. John considers [[stories about Bill] interesting]

Here both brackets are maximal projections but neither is a barrier, on our assumptions. The question arises, then, whether government is possible into the embedded subject NP, as it would be if this were an ordinary object: for example, can the head and specifier of the embedded subject NP be governed from the outside? Assuming the *ne*-extraction theory of Belletti and Rizzi 1981, the answer would seem to be that the head can be governed from the outside, as illustrated by such examples as (199) (due to Rizzi):

(199)

a. ne ritengo [[molti e] intelligenti]

b. of-them I-believe [[many e] intelligent] (I consider many of them intelligent)

We may also ask whether noun incorporation is possible from the embedded subject to the matrix verb; if so, then again we must conclude that it is a single barrier, not two maximal projections, that block government. For examples illustrating this possibility, see Baker 1985.

Turning to case (ii)—adjunct movement over a single maximal projection that is a barrier—consider again such examples as (66b,d):

(200)

it is time [$_{CP}$ for John to [$_{VP}$ fix the car how]]

Here the adjunct *how* adjoins to VP and then moves to the specifier position of CP, crossing no barriers, so that the ECP is satisfied in the intermediate form (201):

(201)

it is time [$_{CP}$ how for John to [$_{VP'}$ t' [$_{VP}$ fix the car t]]]

But further extraction of *how,* yielding (202), is impossible, though it crosses only the single maximal projection CP, a barrier since it is not L-marked:

(202)

*how is it time [for John to fix the car t]

Again, this indicates that it is a single barrier, not two maximal projections, that block government.

The discussion of (198) and similar constructions indicates that in the respects considered, the subject of an embedded non-CP complement behaves in the manner of an object of its verbal governor, and this is quite generally the case. The distinction between the constructions is motivated on more indirect and rather theory-internal grounds. The presumed structural difference does, however, appear to have some direct empirical consequences, noted in the literature.[58] To take another case, consider such constructions as (203a–b), where α is as in (204):

(203)

a. I convinced (encouraged,...) Bill and me [$_{CP}$ to α]

b. I expected (wanted,...) [$_{IP}$ Bill and me to α]

(204)

try harder, become friends, exchange gifts, work together more effectively, . . .

Though the distinction is not sharp, nevertheless (203a) appears less acceptable than (203b) throughout. The distinction might be explained on the assumption that the conjunction is a (possibly somewhat defective) governor of its conjuncts, in which case IP in (203b) would be the governing category for *me*—the minimal complete functional complex (with a subject) containing a governor of *me*—so that the pronoun satisfies binding condition B, whereas the governing category in (203a) would be the whole clause so that condition B is violated, assuming here the version of the binding theory in Chomsky 1985.

The theory outlined earlier still allows illicit movement in a number of cases. One, noted by Andrew Barss, concerns structures such as (205):

(205)

*who do you think [$_{CP}$ that [t [$_{VP}$ likes Bill]]]

I analyzed this as an ECP violation resulting from the Minimality Condition, but Barss observes that an unwanted derivation has not yet been excluded, in which *who* is adjoined to the lower VP, yielding (206), then raised to the specifier of CP, and finally raised to its matrix position:

(206)

*who do you think [$_{CP}$ that [t [$_{VP}$ t' [$_{VP}$ likes Bill]]]]

In (206) *t'* governs (hence, antecedent-governs) *t*, voiding the ECP violation. We might bar this derivation by assuming that antecedent government requires not only m-command but the stronger requirement of c-command in terms of branching (see note 48). For further analysis, considering many other cases as well, see Barss 1985.

---

13. Summary

This discussion has touched on issues related to various components of UG, particularly the theories of government and bounding. We now review briefly the basic ideas examined.

A two-level X-bar theory is extended to the nonlexical categories I and C heading the clausal maximal projections (X^{max}) IP and CP. The theory of movement allows two options, substitution and adjunction, the latter forming categories with several segments. Adjunction is permitted only to nonarguments, perhaps a consequence of θ-theory, and is limited to X^{max} as moved elements or targets.

A head α θ-governs its complements, which it θ-marks; if lexical, α L-marks its complements and their heads. By SPEC-head agreement, θ-government is extended to specifier of IP and CP. These notions are defined in terms of X-bar theory and θ-theory, independently of government.

α governs β if α m-commands β and no barriers for β exclude α. Movement is optimal when it crosses no barriers, and it degrades sharply with crossing of more than one barrier, where "crossing" (like government) is construed in terms of exclusion. Thus, chain links meet the Subjacency Condition, yielding the standard island effects with some low-level parametric variation, including the option of nonmovement in syntax where movement is vacuous. Case-marking and selection take place under government, as does θ-marking, with a strict Sisterhood Condition in the latter case.

Barriers are determined in two ways: (i) on the basis of L-marking, and (ii) by the Minimality Condition. Only the former are relevant for movement. Under (i), an X^{max} γ is a barrier by inheritance or inherently. γ is a barrier by inheritance if the X^{max} it most closely dominates is a blocking category (BC); it is a barrier inherently if it is a BC itself. An X^{max} is a BC if it is not L-marked. Under (ii), a category γ is a barrier for β if it is the immediate projection (alternatively, a projection) of a zero-level category $\delta \neq \beta$. In either case β is not governed by α if α is excluded by a barrier for β. The I-projection system is "defective" in that I' and IP are barriers only by inheritance (so that, in particular, IP is not a barrier for antecedent government and I' is excluded from the Minimality Condition).

Movement may take place in any component and may involve X^{max} or X^0. Certain operators, including *wh*-phrases, cannot adjoin to IP and must be in the specifier position of CP at LF. An operation of chain composition links chains under a condition of anti-c-command, derivable from other principles, or perhaps a condition of 0-subjacency, yielding the parasitic gap phenomenon.

The ECP requires that trace be properly governed—that is, not only governed but also antecedent-governed or, perhaps, θ-governed. The latter option may be void at least for verb-complement structures, perhaps more generally, so that the ECP reduces to a chain property.

The ECP is in effect determined at S-Structure for A-positions and at LF for adjuncts, perhaps as a consequence of the Projection Principle.

The ECP requires that X^0 can only raise to the position of a θ-governor of its X^{max}. NP-movement satisfies the ECP in extended chains, on the assumption of uniqueness of indexing for chains and SPEC-head agreement, and head-head agreement for I and VP, including aspectual elements that select but do not θ-mark VP.

Notes

1. Prime notation is used here rather than bar notation, for typographical reasons: $\overline{X} = X'$, $\overline{\overline{X}} = X''$, and so forth. Nonetheless, I retain the term *X-bar theory*.

2. For various concrete proposals, see among others Stowell 1981, Koopman 1984, and Travis 1984.

3. For a particular (core) language L, the X-bar system is determined by fixing the values of the parameters of X-bar theory (head-first, etc.) in accordance with whatever dependencies among them are determined by UG; a particular set of choices constitutes the X-bar component of the grammar of L. Since there is no known reason to suspect that there are more than a few such parameters, the number of base (X-bar) systems for core grammar appears to be not only finite but in fact small. Note that the question of the length of realizations of X^* in rules does not arise, since there are no such rules in an X-bar system. There will indeed be realizations of the schemata, each dependent on the valuation of parameters for L and the choice of lexical items, under the Projection Principle, but these realizations are no more part of the grammar than each sentence is. Of course, from the fact that the number of possible X-bar systems is finite, indeed small, it does not follow that the number of possible phrase structure systems (including lexicon and marked periphery) is finite, but these possibilities are of slight interest. See Chomsky 1981:11.

There remain open questions of X-bar theory concerning the internal structure of major categories, the nature and status of extraposed elements and minor categories (possibly a matter of lexical features rather than a part of X-bar theory), and other matters, but there is, again, no known reason to suspect that however these are resolved, the variety of possible systems will be large. In the absence of compelling evidence to resolve these empirical questions, there is no point in specifying one or another of the possible options in detail; in particular, further formalization is pointless, since there are no theorems of any interest to be proved or hidden assumptions to be teased out in these systems. The interesting questions have to do with issues of fact.

4. For discussion of such possibilities, see among other works Whitman 1982, Hale 1983, Kiss 1985.

5. Perhaps derived from the theory of predication in the sense of Williams 1980, along lines suggested in Rothstein 1983.

6. Lasnik observes in work in progress that the stronger condition is motivated by the impossibility of *who thinks that who, I like, if (as he argues) structures such as Bill thinks that John, I like are derived by adjunction to IP.

7. Assuming here only one specifier position in CP. On V-raising, see section 11.

8. Fiengo and Higginbotham (1981) argue for QR-adjunction to N' on the basis of scopal properties of such phrases as many people's pictures, pictures of many people. I will assume that this option is excluded for the processes considered here.

9. Lasnik and Uriagereka (1985) note that the argument is problematic, since the device proposed would not suffice to overcome the Bijection Principle violation in such cases as every student asked some actress he met about some play she played in. See also Williams 1977.

10. Formalization of this idea is fairly straightforward, requiring introduction of the notion of occurrence of a category.

11. For various specific definitions and considerations bearing on them, see Reinhart 1976, Aoun and Sportiche 1983, Chomsky 1981, and references cited in those works. Assume domination to be irreflexive.

12. We may assume that β does not dominate α in (13), to exclude m-command by X of its projection X'. We might also exclude self-command, permitted here.

13. I will tentatively assume this analysis, though it raises problems noted below and is not consistent with conclusions reached in section 11.

14. Note that it is the given interpretations of (22b,d) that are excluded; that is, the sentences can be understood only with how associated with the matrix verb, as distinct from (22a).

15. See Chomsky 1985 and references cited for further discussion.

16. Direct θ-marking by a lexical head is sometimes called "lexical government"; we will reserve the latter term for government by a lexical category whether or not a θ-role is assigned.

17. Higginbotham (1983, 1985) argues that coindexing should be replaced by an asymmetric notion of linking in binding theory, hence in chains. The concepts developed here can readily be restated in these terms.

18. This is a considerable improvement over the analysis in Chomsky 1981 in terms of Subjacency. A binding-theoretic explanation is dubious, since pleonastics yield only "weak" violations. In unpublished work Giuseppe Longobardi provides further evidence that this is not the right approach.

19. I follow here observations by Luigi Rizzi (personal communication). If I θ-marks VP, then θ-theory will have to ensure that NP is not a proper recipient for the θ-role assigned by I. On extension of Case theory to include verbs as recipients, see Fabb 1984.

20. Thus, t, in this case, would be an $\bar{\text{A}}$-bound R-expression that is A-bound in the domain of the head of its chain, violating condition C of the binding theory. For discussion, see Chomsky 1981, 1985.

21. Only the case of L-marking of specifier is relevant here; on L-marking of head, see section 12.

22. As argued, for example, by Fabb (1984) and Hornstein and Lightfoot (1984).

23. For example, it motivates various proposed conventions regarding COMP-indexing by *wh*-phrase.

24. I follow here suggestions by Luigi Rizzi and Mark Ryser.

25. I put aside here the question whether Subjacency is a condition on movement or on the resulting representation.

26. On parsing-theoretic motivation for a subjacency condition, see Berwick and Weinberg 1983, 1985.

27. Belletti reports that in Italian only the (nonstranding) relative cases are acceptable.

28. Howard Lasnik (personal communication) notes that the empty head of the embedded CP is not properly governed here, one of a number of questions concerning proper government of the head of an infinitival clause and more generally concerning an account for the distribution of empty C in terms of proper government. See section 11.

29. Consider, for example, such cases as (i)–(iii), all relatively acceptable cases of multiple *wh*-questions:

(i)   who thinks that [pictures of whom] are on sale
(ii) who left [before doing what]
(iii) who thinks that [for whom to do what] would be a mistake

See also Huang 1982.

30. One might argue that the examples differ in this regard, (72a) at least being a kind of "appositive" construction in the sense discussed in Stowell 1981.

31. See Chomsky 1985 for discussion concerning a Case theory of this sort. Note that in this system *of* realizes oblique Case in (72c), but the *of*-phrase itself need not be assumed to have Case so as to constitute a barrier.

32. Independently of this, a crossing effect may reduce the acceptability of (77a,c) as compared to (77b,d).

33. Larson provides evidence that *before* selects what we are considering to be the specifier of its clausal complement, thus strengthening the argument that government holds between α and the specifier of its complement.

34. If VP-fronting too is a PF rule, the question of proper government in such cases as (38) would be voided.

35. Assume here that in accordance with X-bar theory, nouns have the same complement structure as verbs, and that *of* is the realization of Case; see Chomsky 1981, 1985 for further references and details.

36. There might, however, be Case-theoretic consequences under other conditions, for example, if the matrix verb had an extra Case to assign or if the NP object could escape the Case Filter in a different way. For discussion of such possibilities, see Baker 1985, Massam 1985.

37. But *see* does not L-mark *Bill* in this case, since SPEC-head agreement does not hold between the specifier and the head of the NP in (93).

38. For further discussion over a broader range of constructions, see Cinque 1980, Torrego 1985, and references cited.

39. More specifically, that it lacks ϕ-features; see section 5.

40. The case would then be analogous to (106b), where at LF a trace of *how* is not properly governed by *how* (or its trace) in the specifier position of the embedded CP.

41. Independently, the Minimality Condition induces an ECP effect, as in the case of (95).

42. This restriction might be too strong for UG, however; thus, it is inconsistent with the analysis that Lasnik and Saito present for Polish. Perhaps the multiple *wh*-movement they discuss can in part be assigned to the PF component.

43. We interpret (117) to permit movement through any specifier position as long as the *wh*-phrase ultimately reaches a position occupied by *wh*-. Lasnik and Saito give an analysis of (114e) in these terms.

44. For discussion of basic properties of this construction, see Taraldsen 1981, Engdahl 1983, Chomsky 1982, Kayne 1984, and Pesetsky 1982, among others.

45. (144) must be interpreted with *warn* transitive; otherwise, the example is irrelevant. The problem is overcome with a pure transitive such as *convince* in place of *warn*, but now the sentence seems less acceptable (Richard Hudson, personal communication).

46. On the status of such a condition, see Chomsky 1985.

47. Note that subjacency does not entail c-command.

48. See Baker 1985 for extensive discussion. One illicit derivation still admitted here would be raising of the head of NP to V_I formed by V-raising to I in a CP-deletion structure such as (i), where NP is L-marked by V':

(i) ...V' [$_{IP}$ NP [$_{I'}$ V_I VP]]

Perhaps antecedent government requires not merely m-command but the stronger requirement of c-command (see sections 3 and 12). I assume that in the configuration (i), the head of NP could raise to V'.

49. See Travis 1984. Recall that movement of head to specifier is barred; see (4).

50. We might assume, then, that the head-marking properties of I block percolation of the head-marking properties of V to V_I.

51. The latter conclusion appears to be necessary for the copula, as we will see directly.

52. It is barred, independently, since the variable lacks Case, but the analogous construction *who does John believe to be intelligent* is permitted, with VP-adjunction.

53. Essentially the same convention is assumed, in slightly different terms, in the theory outlined in Chomsky 1981 and related work.

54. If we adopt this assumption, then VP must be assumed to be exempt from the θ-Criterion if the argument of section 4 (see discussion of (29)) concerning (6) is to go through; that is, VP may be but need not be θ-marked by I.

55. Alternatively, that the AP is not a complement of the copula, as proposed by Longobardi (1984).

56. See Chomsky 1975 for discussion of the possibility that *pick-clean,* and so forth, are complex verbs.

57. See Demonte 1985 for further discussion.

58. See, for example, the discussion in Chomsky 1981:99–100, following Mark Baltin; also see Pesetsky 1982.

References

Aoun, J., and D. Sportiche (1983). "On the Formal Theory of Government." *The Linguistic Review* 3, 211–235.

Baker, C. L. (1970). "Notes on the Description of English Questions." *Foundations of Language* 6, 197–219.

Baker, M. (1985). *Incorporation: A Theory of Grammatical Function Changing*. Doctoral dissertation, MIT.

Barss, A. (1985). "Adjunction and Reflexive Hierarchical Relations." Ms., MIT.

Belletti, A., and L. Rizzi (1981). "The Syntax of 'ne': Some Theoretical Implications." *The Linguistic Review* 1, 117–154.

Berwick, R., and A. Weinberg (1983). *The Grammatical Basis of Linguistic Performance*. MIT Press, Cambridge, Mass.

Berwick, R., and A. Weinberg (1985). "Deterministic Parsing and Linguistic Explanation." *Language and Cognitive Processes* 1.2.

Bouchard, D. (1984). *On the Content of Empty Categories*. Foris, Dordrecht.

Brody, M. (1984). "On Contextual Definitions and the Role of Chains." *Linguistic Inquiry* 15, 355–381.

Cattell, R. (1976). "Constraints on Movement Rules." *Language* 52, 18–50.

Chomsky, N. (1964). *Current Issues in Linguistic Theory*. The Hague, Mouton.

Chomsky, N. (1975). *The Logical Structure of Linguistic Theory*. Plenum, New York. [Also 1985, University of Chicago Press.]

Chomsky, N. (1981). *Lectures on Government and Binding*. Foris, Dordrecht.

Chomsky, N. (1982). *Some Concepts and Consequences of the Theory of Government and Binding*. MIT Press, Cambridge, Mass.

Chomsky, N. (1985). *Knowledge of Language: Its Nature, Origin and Use*. New York, Praeger.

Chung, S., and J. McCloskey (1983). "On the Interpretation of Certain Island Facts in GPSG." *Linguistic Inquiry* 14, 704–713.

Cinque, G. (1980). "On Extraction from NP in Italian." *Journal of Italian Linguistics* 5, 47–99.

Contreras, H. (1984). "A Note on Parasitic Gaps." *Linguistic Inquiry* 15, 704–713.

Culicover, P., and W. Wilkins (1984). *Locality in Linguistic Theory.* Academic Press, New York.

Demonte, V. (1985). "On Adjectival Predication." Ms., Universidad Autónoma, Madrid, and MIT.

Emonds, J. (1976). *A Transformational Approach to English Syntax.* Academic Press, New York.

Engdahl, E. (1983). "Parasitic Gaps." *Linguistics and Philosophy* 6, 5–34.

Engdahl, E. (1984). "Parasitic Gaps, Resumptive Pronouns, and Subject Extractions." Ms., University of Wisconsin, Madison.

Fabb, N. (1984). *Syntactic Affixation.* Doctoral dissertation, MIT.

Fiengo, R., and J. Higginbotham (1981). "Opacity in NP." *Linguistic Analysis* 7, 395–422.

George, L. (1980). *Analogical Generalization in Natural Language Syntax.* Doctoral dissertation, MIT.

Hale, K. (1983). "Warlpiri and the Grammar of Non-configurational Languages." *Natural Language & Linguistic Theory* 1, 5–47.

Higginbotham, J. (1983). "Logical Form, Binding, and Nominals." *Linguistic Inquiry* 14, 395–420.

Higginbotham, J. (1985). "On Semantics." *Linguistic Inquiry* 16, 547–593.

Higginbotham, J., and R. May (1981). "Questions, Quantifiers, and Crossing." *The Linguistic Review* 1, 41–79.

Hornstein, N., and D. Lightfoot (1984). "Rethinking Predication." Ms., University of Maryland.

Huang, C.-T. J. (1982). *Logical Relations in Chinese and the Theory of Grammar.* Doctoral dissertation, MIT.

Hudson, R. (1984). "Multiple (Alias 'Parasitic') Gaps." Ms., University College London.

Kayne, R. (1984). *Connectedness and Binary Branching.* Foris, Dordrecht.

Kearney, K. (1983). "Governing Categories." Ms., University of Connecticut, Storrs.

Kiss, K. (1985). "Is the VP Universal?" Ms., MIT.

Koopman, H. (1984). *The Syntax of Verbs*. Foris, Dordrecht.

Koopman, H., and D. Sportiche (1982). "Variables and the Bijection Principle." *The Linguistic Review* 2, 139–160.

Koster, J. (1978). *Locality Principles in Syntax*. Foris, Dordrecht.

Kuno, S. (1972). "Functional Sentence Perspective." *Linguistic Inquiry* 3, 269–320.

Larson, R. (1983). "Extraction and Double Selection in PP." Ms., MIT.

Lasnik, H., and M. Saito (1984). "On the Nature of Proper Government." *Linguistic Inquiry* 15, 235–289.

Lasnik, H., and J. Uriagereka (1985). *Lectures on Binding and Government: A Second Semester Syntax Course*. Ms., University of Connecticut, Storrs.

Longobardi, G. (1984). "Su alcune proprietà della sintassi e della forma logica delle frasi copulari." Ms., Scuola Normale Superiore, Pisa.

Longobardi, G. (forthcoming). "The Theoretical Status of the Adjunct Condition."

Marantz, A. (1984). *On the Nature of Grammatical Relations*. MIT Press, Cambridge, Mass.

Massam, D. (1985). *Case Theory and the Projection Principle*. Doctoral dissertation, MIT.

May, R. (1985). *Logical Form*. MIT Press, Cambridge, Mass.

Montalbetti, M. (1984). *After Binding*. Doctoral dissertation, MIT.

Pesetsky, D. (1981). "Complementizer-Trace Phenomena and the Nominative Island Condition." *The Linguistic Review* 1, 297–343.

Pesetsky, D. (1982). *Paths and Categories*. Doctoral dissertation, MIT.

Reinhart, T. (1976). *The Syntactic Domain of Anaphora*. Doctoral dissertation, MIT.

Rizzi, L. (1982). *Issues in Italian Syntax*. Foris, Dordrecht.

Rizzi, L. (1984). *Spegazione e Teoria Grammaticale*. CLESP, Padua.

Ross, J. R. (1967). *Constraints on Variables in Syntax*. Doctoral dissertation, MIT.

Ross, J. R. (1983). "Reciflexives and Extraposition from *Picture*-Nouns." Ms., MIT and University of the Air.

Rothstein, S. (1983). *The Syntactic Forms of Predication*. Doctoral dissertation, MIT.

Rouveret, A., and J.-R. Vergnaud (1980). "Specifying Reference to the Subject: French Causatives and Conditions and Representations." *Linguistic Inquiry* 11, 97–202.

Saito, M. (1984). "Three Notes on Syntactic Movement in Japanese." Ms., MIT.

Sportiche, D. (1981). "Bounding Nodes in French." *The Linguistic Review* 1, 219–246.

Stowell, T. (1981). *Origins of Phrase Structure*. Doctoral dissertation, MIT.

Stowell, T. (1983). "Subjects across Categories." *The Linguistic Review* 2, 285–312.

Taraldsen, K. T. (1981). "The Theoretical Interpretation of a Class of Marked Extractions." In A. Belletti, L. Brandi, and L. Rizzi, eds., *Theory of Markedness in Generative Grammar, Proceedings of the 1979 GLOW Conference*, 475–516. Scuola Normale Superiore, Pisa.

Torrego, E. (1985). "On Empty Categories in Nominals." Ms., University of Massachusetts, Boston.

Travis, L. (1984). *Parameters and Effects of Word Order Variation*. Doctoral dissertation, MIT.

Vergnaud, J.-R. (1982). *Dépendances et niveaux de représentation en syntaxe*. Thèse de Doctorat d'Etat, Université de Paris VII.

Whitman, J. (1982). "Configurationality Parameters." Ms., Harvard University.

Williams, E. (1977). "Discourse and Logical Form." *Linguistic Inquiry* 8, 103–139.

Williams, E. (1980). "Predication." *Linguistic Inquiry* 11, 203–238.

Index